John Paul Jones' Memoir

John Paul Jones

craindre qu'il ne se cassât au-dessous du pont, ou qu'il ne creusât un trou dans le fond de la Frégate? je le fis couper, et dans sa chûte, il entraina le mât d'artimon et la galère du quart.

Dans cette Situation l'Ariel tint l'ancre, en pleine mer, au vent et Sur le bord des Rocs les plus dangéreux du monde, pendant deux jours et trois nuits; dans une tempête qui couvrit le rivage de naufrages, et qui chassa les Vaisseaux amarés même dans le Port de l'Orient. Il est à présumer que jamais auparavant, Vaisseau ne se Sauva de pareilles circonstances.

Je fis mettre les mâts de nécessité après la tempête, et je retournai à Lorient, d'où je m'adressai à M. de Castries, alors devenu Ministre de la Marine, pour le prier d'échanger l'Ariel contre la Frégate Terpsicore, ce que je ne pus obtenir. Je fus donc retenu à Lorient pour remâter l'Ariel jusqu'au 18 Décembre 1780. que je mis en mer pour Philadelphie. Comme j'étois chargé des Dépêches de la Cour pendant six mois pour M. le Chevalier de la Luzerne, la Flotte françoise et l'armée qui étois en Amérique, je ne Souhaitai point de rencontrer l'ennemi dans mon passage; j'envisageai

John Paul Jones' Memoir
of the American Revolution

PRESENTED TO
KING LOUIS XVI OF FRANCE

Translated and Edited by
Gerard W. Gawalt

With an Introduction by
John R. Sellers

American Revolution Bicentennial Office

LIBRARY OF CONGRESS   WASHINGTON   1979

Library of Congress Cataloging in Publication Data

Jones, John Paul, 1747-1792.
  John Paul Jones' Memoir of the American Revolution presented to King Louis XVI of
France.

  Translation of a manuscript entitled: Extrait du journal de mes campagnes, où j'expose mes
principaux services et rappelle quelques circonstances de ce qui m'est arrivé de plus remarquable
pendant le cours de la Révolution-américaine, particulièrement en Europe.
  Includes bibliographical references.
  1. Jones, John Paul, 1747-1792. 2. United States—History—Revolution, 1775-1783—
Naval operations. 3. United States—History—Revolution, 1775-1783—Personal narratives.
4. Admirals—United States—Biography. I. Gawalt, Gerard W. II. Sellers, John R. III.
Title. IV. Title: Memoir of the American Revolution presented to King Louis XVI of
France.
E207.J7A34   973.3'5'0924   78-6650
ISBN 0-8444-0264-8

For sale by the Superintendent of Documents, U.S. Government Printing Office, Washington,
D. C. 20402. When ordering cite the publisher (Library of Congress), title, and stock number
(S/N 030-000-00094-3). Payment must accompany order.

CONTENTS

ILLUSTRATIONS

ACKNOWLEDGMENTS

Special thanks are due to Madame Ulane Bonnel, the Library of Congress déléguée in Paris, for her aid and advice as well as for the vital information she secured from French archives. The translator is also obliged to P. C. Soeters, head of the Department of Dutch History, Koninklijke Bibliotheek, The Hague, Netherlands, and Nathalie P. Delougaz, chief, Shared Cataloging Division, Library of Congress, for their assistance in this project.

Gerard W. Gawalt

TRANSLATOR'S NOTE

Editorial guidelines for this publication are in accordance with the modern method of editing with suitable flexibility to meet the needs of a work that includes both a translated section and one of 18th-century English texts. The translation was designed to produce a readable English version that adheres to the original, 18th-century meaning and flavor expressed by the author. For this reason the editor did not alter spellings of personal and geographic names. Errors in fact committed by John Paul Jones have been left uncorrected in the text.

In Jones' transmittal letter to the king and in the English texts appended as documentary evidence the editor has held to a middle course between the poles of a facsimile version and a complete modernization. The requirements of literal reproduction are often impossible to fulfill, and a limited degree of conventionalization is often desirable for clarity. Capital and lowercase letters were preserved as found, except that each sentence in the printed text begins with a capital. The original punctuation has been kept, with terminal punctuation supplied when necessary. Abbreviations and contractions have been expanded only when helpful in clarifying meaning. Superscript letters have been brought down to the line.

A glossary of people prominently mentioned in the text has been used to supplement the footnotes, which have been added only when necessary for understanding the author's meaning. The editor has provided analytical comments and cross-references to secondary or manuscript materials whenever they contribute significantly to a fuller understanding of Jones' revolutionary war career.

INTRODUCTION

Anyone familiar with the life of John Paul Jones, one of America's most popular naval heroes, would agree that in fighting spirit the commodore was perhaps equal to any officer in the history of the United States Navy. Unquestionably, he was deserving of the belated tribute paid to him by President Theodore Roosevelt on April 24, 1906, at the formal reception at Annapolis of the body of Capt. Paul Jones, as the hero was known at the height of his career. President Roosevelt admonished an audience of naval officers and cadets, statesmen, and visiting dignitaries: "Every officer in our Navy should know by heart the deeds of John Paul Jones. Every officer in our Navy should feel in each fiber of his being an eager desire to emulate the energy, the professional capacity, the indomitable determination and dauntless scorn of death which marked John Paul Jones above all his fellows."

Born in 1747 in Kirkbean Parish along the north bank of the Solway Firth, a deep inlet on the western borders of England and Scotland, John Paul developed a love for the sea early in life. At 13 he became apprenticed to a merchant at Whitehaven across the Firth, and before he was 16 he had made several voyages to America and the West Indies on the brig *Friendship*. On at least three separate occasions he visited his older brother William, a tailor at Fredericksburg, Va.

Owing to the financial ruin of his master, John Paul's apprenticeship aboard the *Friendship* was shortened by about three years. He was only on the beach a few weeks, however, before signing up as third mate on a slaver, also out of Whitehaven. But John Paul eventually had enough of that brutal business. In July 1768, while at Kingston, Jamaica, he accepted the offer of a Kirkcudbright man, Capt. Samuel McAdam, of a free passage home on the brig *John* of Liverpool. During the voyage both Captain McAdam and the ship's mate died of a fever, and John Paul, already an accomplished navigator, brought the vessel safely to port. This deed so pleased the owners of the *John* that they appointed him to command the vessel.

At age 21 John Paul was well on the way to a successful career as a merchant skipper. And had it not been for two unfortunate experiences, he might never have shown more than a passing interest in America. In late 1770 on a voyage to the West Indies, Captain Paul, a strict disciplinarian, severely whipped his ship's carpenter, one Mungo Maxwell, son of a prominent Kirkcudbright gentleman. At Tobago Maxwell lodged a formal complaint against John Paul at the vice-admiralty court and then shipped home in the *Barcelona Packet*. There the affair should have ended, because a judge had examined Maxwell's wounds and declared them superficial. But Maxwell died on the return trip, and although his death resulted from a fever and was in no way connected with the flogging, Captain Paul acquired the reputation of a hard taskmaster. Hence on another occasion when John Paul was faced with a mutinous crew while in port at Tobago and killed the ringleader (perhaps inadvertently), he quietly shipped out to America rather than stand trial in a civil court on the island.

Thus John Paul, his name conveniently changed to Paul Jones, took up residence in America at a time when relations between Great Britain and the 13 American colonies were working up to a crisis. With the outbreak of hostilities and the resultant prohibitions on trade and the collection of debts, he was forced to rely on the charity of his American friends. But the little Scotsman was too proud to continue long in that fashion. In the fall of 1775 he suddenly appeared in Philadelphia in response to an announcement that Congress was seeking men to staff the newly established Continental navy. With the aid of Joseph Hewes, delegate from North Carolina and member of the Naval Committee, he was commissioned first lieutenant on the *Alfred*.

The revolutionary career of Jones, which is the subject of this memoir, needs no elaboration here. His voyages, first on the *Alfred* under Capt. Dudley Saltonstall, and later at the helm of the sloops *Providence*, *Ranger*, and *Ariel*, the old East Indiaman *Duras* (renamed the *Bonhomme Richard*), and the American-built frigate *Alliance* are thoroughly recounted in the succeeding pages. What is generally not known, however, is the commodore's post-revolutionary war career. Having made numerous inveterate enemies during the course of the war, both in and out of Congress, Jones had little chance of gaining flag rank in the American navy. Realizing this, he decided in the spring of 1788 to pursue fame in other waters, first in the service of Louis XVI of France and later under Catherine the Great of Russia. France, unfortunately, was in no position to expand its naval staff, but Catherine, who was in need of good officers to fight in the second Russo-Turkish war, offered him an admiral's commission in the Russian navy, and on May 26, 1788, Rear Admiral Jones raised his flag on the Black Sea.

If the Turks had been the only enemies Jones encountered in his Russian tour, he doubtless would have reached new heights in his amazing career. Instead, he fell victim to the jealous intrigues of his old rival, the French adventurer Prince Nassau-Siegen, and was sidelined for much of the war. In September 1789 he left St. Petersburg under a cloud of personal and professional humiliation, and following a sojourn in Holland of about five months, he arrived in Paris a ghost of a man at age 42.

No longer the man of the hour, his spirits sagging, his uniform fading, and all but forgotten in the bustle of the French Revolution, the commodore lingered on in Paris for two more years writing letters he hoped would regain him the favor of former benefactors. At regular intervals he visited the American legation to chat with Gouverneur Morris, American minister to France. Finally, knowing that death was imminent, on the afternoon of July 18, 1792, Jones called Morris to his bedside to record his will. He died later that same afternoon unaware that on June 2 President Washington had appointed him American consul for Algeria.

Jones' funeral was a far cry from the final salute Americans have traditionally reserved for men of such stature. In fact, the once proud commander barely escaped being cast in a pauper's grave, because Morris, acting under a conviction that he had no right to spend public money on funerals, had left orders with Jones' landlord to have the commodore's body put away as privately and economically as possible. It was only by chance that the matter was taken out of the hands of Morris and a more fitting ceremony arranged.

The funeral began about 7 o'clock on the evening of July 20, 1792, two days after the commodore's death. Leading the procession was a small detachment of French grenadiers, followed by a hearse, and a 12-man deputation from the Assemblée législative. After the assemblymen marched a delegation from the Protestants of Paris with their pastor, the Reverend Paul-Henri Marron, the man appointed to deliver the funeral oration, followed by several members of the Lodge of Nine Sisters and, finally, a small coterie of friends and admirers. Marching in mournful cadence, this small cortège wound its way through the streets of Paris, past the city gates, and on to the Cemetery of St. Louis, the official burial ground for Protestants.

Across the Atlantic few people were concerned with their debt to Jones, and no effort was made to remove his remains to this country or even to maintain the gravesite. It fell to eminent writers like Herman Melville, James Fenimore Cooper, and Rudyard Kipling, along with a few solicitous biographers, to keep his fame alive until the nation was ready to pay him his just acclaim. But toward the end of the 19th century, the commodore's unusual exploits in the war of the Revolution, which by then had been heralded by poets, novelists, and historians alike, captured the imagination of Americans, and a search for his body was begun. This grisly task involved extensive excavation in a long-abandoned cemetery, but on April 7, 1905, Gen. Horace Porter, then American ambassador to France, unearthed the remains. To the relief of all concerned, Jones' corpse was so well preserved that it was easily identified by two eminent anthropologists, who compared it with a 1780 bust of Jones made from life by Jean-Antoine Houdon. Three months later the body was brought to the United States under naval escort, where it received fitting tribute. Today the commodore's remains lie permanently encased in a marble sarcophagus at the Naval Academy Chapel.

Despite this belated recognition, neglect still surrounds a significant item in the life of John Paul Jones—his autobiography. In late 1785, on the occasion of a threatened renewal of hostilities between England and France, Jones drafted a manuscript entitled in the king's copy: "Extrait du Journal des Services principaux De Paul-Jones, dans la Révolution des Etats-Unis D'Amerique; écrit par lui-même, et presenté avec un profond respect, au Trés illustre Prince Louis XVI." Essentially, this document provides a detailed and highly colored account of Jones' service in the Continental navy. His unstated, but undeniable purpose was to persuade the king of France that he was worthy of an admiral's commission in the French royal navy.

Jones used every ploy at his disposal in his efforts to win a place in the royal navy, even to reminding the king of the great confidence the Crown had formerly professed to have in him. Also, to encourage the king to read the document for himself, he hired a secretary, Benoit André, to translate it into French. Jones was aware that the king possessed considerable knowledge of the English language, but he evidently was taking no chances.

Jones had his secretary make at least four French copies of the autobiography: one for the king; one for the comte de Vergennes, the French foreign minister; one for the marquis de Castries, the minister of marine; and one for himself. Of these four, only the copy Jones presented to Louis XVI after his return to France in December 1787 and Jones' personal copy have survived. Even the English original has disappeared, although Robert C. Sands claimed to have included extracts, with Jones' annotations, in his *Life and Correspondence of John Paul Jones* (1830). Both remaining French copies are bound in red morocco with the royal arms of France emblazoned on the front covers. The presentation copy, which has a more elaborate ornamentation, is in the Archives nationales, Archives de la marine (MM851). Jones' own copy is with the John Paul Jones Papers in the Library of Congress. An incomplete English retranslation of the Jones memoir, entitled *An Account of the Celebrated Commodore Paul Jones: Translated From a Manuscript, Written by Himself*, was published in 1806 by Peter K. Wagner and reprinted in installments in Niles' *Weekly Register* 2 (May–July 1812).

The two surviving French copies of the memoir are almost identical, the main difference being in the number and selection of commendatory letters appended to each. Jones' copy, for example, contains transcriptions of 45 letters, whereas the presentation copy contains only 36. A letter that Benjamin Franklin sent Jones in 1779 on the subject of American prisoners in England was also copied on the last page of the king's volume, but it is in a different hand and technically not a part of the document. Among the correspondents represented in the additional nine letters in Jones' copy are Robert Morris, the comte d'Estaing, and John Jay, who wrote in behalf of the Continental Congress. In 1798 André had the manuscript published in French as the *Mémoires de Paul Jones, où il expose ses principaux services, et rappelle ce qui lui est arrivé de plus remarquable pendant le cours de la révolution américaine, particulièrement en Europe, escrits par lui-même en anglais, et traduits sous ses yeux par le citoyen André*. Never reprinted, the Paris edition is now quite rare. The translation of the manuscript at the Library of Congress which follows is believed to be the first complete English edition of the memoir.

In judging the quality of a work of this kind there are certain points that should not be overlooked, the most crucial one being that the narrative does not always conform to some of the known facts about events in which Jones was involved. Ordinarily such deficiencies would impair the usefulness of a book, but in this instance what appears at first glance to be a major flaw is really an asset. Jones was a blatant egotist, seldom able to examine an issue from a perspective other than his own, and not above twisting the record for personal advantage. Hence his occasional prevarications, his failures to provide information on the men who served under his command or the places he visited, his neglect of incidents that might cast him in a bad light, and the absence of personal items all serve to provide the reader with an almost perfect reflection.

On the positive side, however, the commodore's strengths are as readily apparent as his foibles. Who can help but be impressed that despite inexperienced crews, inferior ships, and inadequate artillery, the commodore won some of the most spectacular battles ever fought on the high sea? For sheer courage, seamanship, and fighting ability, John Paul Jones was second to none.

According to Jones' will, dated at Paris on the day of his death, his property and effects were to go to his sisters in Scotland. Except for his voluminous correspondence, however, there was little worth claiming. An early Jones biographer states that the commodore's papers were taken to Scotland by his eldest sister late in 1792, and, from the best evidence available, it appears that most of the items relating to the American Revolution were sent to the United States in 1797 at the request of Robert Hyslop, a family friend living in New York City. Hyslop may have obtained the papers to support claims against the United States by Jones' heirs. In 1830 a second group of papers was brought into the country by Jones' niece, Janette Taylor of Dumfries, Scotland, but the memoir with which we are here concerned probably was a part of the papers acquired by Hyslop. Hyslop retained possession of these materials until his death, at which time they fell into the hands of his cousin and executor, John Hyslop, also of New York. The next person known to have possessed them was George A. Ward. Ward knew something of their value, but by then several important items, such as the logbooks kept by Jones on board the *Ranger*, the *Bonhomme Richard*, the *Serapis*, the *Alliance*, and *l'Ariel*, had been sold. The remaining documents eventually were acquired by Peter Force, whose historic collection was purchased for the Library of Congress by special act of Congress, March 2, 1867.

Today John Paul Jones symbolizes the fighting spirit of America's revolutionary generation. It is especially appropriate, therefore, for the Library of Congress to publish, as a contribution to the Bicentennial observance, this personal account of his career in the Continental navy. On the eve of the 200th anniversary of the defeat of the *Serapis* by the *Bonhomme Richard*, Jones' memoir serves as a reminder of the Library's rich manuscript holdings from the period of the American Revolution.

John R. Sellers
American Revolution
Bicentennial Office

John Paul Jones' Memoir of the American Revolution

PRESENTED TO
KING LOUIS XVI OF FRANCE

Sire,

History gives the World no example of such Gene-
rosity as that of your Majesty towards the young
Republic of America; and I beleive there never was a
Compliment more flattering shewn by a Sovereing to his
Allies, than when your Majesty determined to Arm and
support a squadron under the Flag of the United States.

Words cannot express my sense of the preference I
obtained when your Majesty deigned to make choice of
me to command that squadron.

Your Majesty has as much Reputation for Knowledge
and the desire of information, as you have for Wisdom
and Justice; but besides that consideration, I conceive it
to be my duty to lay before your Majesty an account of
my conduct as an officer, particularly, from the date
of the Alliance between your Majesty, and the United
States. As your Majesty understands English, I have
perhaps judged ill by presenting the extracts of my
Journals in French; my motive was to give your
Majesty as little trouble as possible.

Accept, Sire, with indulgence this Confidential
offering of my Gratitude; Which is an Original Written
for you particular information.

It has been and will be the ambition of my Life

Sire,

History gives the World no example of such Generosity as that of your Majesty towards the young Republic of America; and I beleive there never was a Compliment more flattering shewn by a Sovereing to his Allies, than when your Majesty determined to Arm and support a Squadron under the Flag of the United-States.

Words cannot express my sense of the preference I obtained, when your Majesty deigned to make choice of me to command that squadron.

Your Majesty has as much Reputation for Knowlidge and the desire of information, as you have for Wisdom and Justice; but besides that consideration, I conceive it to be my duty to lay before your Majesty an account of my conduct as an officier, particularly from the date of the Alliance between your Majesty and the United-States. As your Majesty understands English, I have perhaps judged ill by presenting the extract of my Journals in French: my motive was to give your Majesty as little trouble as possible.

Accept, Sire, with indulgence this Confidential offering of my Gratitude; which is an Original Written for you particular information.

It has been and will be the ambition of my Life to merit the Singular honor confered on me by your Majesty's Brevet dated at Versailles the 28th of June 1780. Which says—"Sa Majesté Voulant marquer au J. Paul-Jones Commodore de la Marine des Etats-Unis de l'Amérique, *l'estime particulière qu'elle fait de sa personne*, pour les preuves de Bravoure et d'Intrépidité qu'il a données et qui sont connues de sa Majesté, elle a jugé à propos de l'associer à l'institution du Mérite Militaire etc."

The Congress of the United-States has, with great justice, stiled your Majesty "The Protector of the Rights of human Nature."

With the Order of Military Merit your Majesty confered on me a Gold Sword: an honor which I presume no other officer has received; and "The Protector of the Rights of human Nature" will always find me ready to draw that Sword and expose my Life for his Service.

> I am, Sire with the truest Gratitude
> Your Majesty's most obliged
> and devoted Servant
> PAUL-JONES

Paris January 1st 1786.

> Protector of fair Freedoms Rights,
> Louis, thy Virtues suit a God!
> The good Man in thy praise delights,
> And Tyrants trimble at thy nod!
>
> Thy peoples Father, lov'd so well,
> May Time respect!—When thou art gone,
> May each new-year of hist'ry tell,
> Thy sons, with lustre fill thy Throne.

Extrait du Journal de mes Campagnes, ou j'expose mes principaux Services et rappelle quelques circonstances de ce qui m'est arrivé de plus remarquable pendant le cours de la *Revolution*—Américaine, particulierement en Europe.

At the beginning of the war, during the year 1775, I was charged with fitting out the small squadron which Congress had placed under the command of Mr. Hopkins, commander of the American navy; and I hoisted with my own hands (on board the *Alfred*, flagship of the commander in chief) the American flag, then unfurled for the first time.[1]

At the same time, I told Mr. Hewes, a member of Congress and my special friend, of a project that afterward was fully planned by the two of us. The goal of this project was to seize the Island of St. Helena and for that purpose to dispatch the fleet against this island, which was very important for America to possess because the vessels of the British East India Company would not fail to drop anchor at that spot on their homeward trip; and in this manner they would inevitably fall into American hands. Because Congress had then proposed to retain two-thirds of the prizes for itself, it would thus have acquired the means to carry on the war for many years. But an event of a more pressing nature prevented this project from being executed.

The depredations and cruelties that the governor, Lord Dunmore, was then inflicting in Virginia determined the Congress to send the squadron against him. Mr. Hopkins displayed neither zeal nor intelligence on this occasion; he lost so much time that his squadron found itself imprisoned by ice in the Delaware.[2] After a two-month delay, the squadron finally was freed and set sail for and seized New Providence, the principal place in the Bahama Islands. There we found a large

---

[1] The banner which Jones raised on the *Alfred* was the so-called Grand Union flag or "Continental Colours," which had a Union Jack on the canton and 13 red and white stripes. There is evidence that the flag was hoisted on December 3, 1775, by Jones while he was "senior of the first lieutenants" assigned to the *Alfred* and acting captain in the absence of the commander, Dudley Saltonstall, who appeared only a day or two before the ships sailed on the New Providence cruise. Hugh F. Rankin, "The Naval Flag of the American Revolution," *William & Mary Quarterly*, 3d ser. 11 (July 1954): 340–41; Samuel Eliot Morison, *John Paul Jones, a Sailor's Biography* (Boston: Little, Brown, 1959), pp. 38–43, 423–25; Lincoln Lorenz, *John Paul Jones, Fighter for Freedom and Glory* (Annapolis, Md.: U. S. Naval Institute, 1943), pp. 59–62.

[2] The fleet was at Reedy Island from January 17 to February 11. William J. Morgan, *Captains to the Northward; the New England Captains in the Continental Navy* (Barre, Mass.: Barre Gazette, 1959), p. 38.

quantity of artillery, mortars, and other implements of war, of which America was in great want. All this materiel was embarked and the governor and officers were taken prisoners, and all were brought to America. During this expedition I had the good fortune to render myself very useful to Mr. Hopkins, who was little acquainted with military operations. It was I who developed the plan that was adopted when the squadron came in sight of New Providence, where I took charge of sailing the squadron into the moorage from which it executed our enterprise.[3]

During our return from New Providence, Mr. Hopkins encountered and captured a small bomb brig and a small armed tender, both ships of war and part of the English navy.[4] These ships were taken without resistance. Shortly after he encountered an English frigate, the *Glasgow* of 24 guns, near Rhode Island; but although he had the advantage of superior power and a favorable wind, he allowed her to escape after suffering many men killed and wounded on board the *Alfred* and the *Cabot*.[5]

The squadron with its prizes entered the port of New London in Connecticut and Mr. Hopkins, upon receiving the news that the English frigates had been driven from Newport, took advantage of the darkness of the night to proceed to Rhode

---

[3] Gov. Montfort Browne managed to ship Fort Nassau's gunpowder off the island literally under the bows of the American ships. Among the captured military supplies were 78 cannons, 15 mortars, and over 16,000 shells and cannon balls. There is no evidence to support Jones' claim that he played a major role in the New Providence operation, and one recent scholar, Nathan Miller, assigns major credit for the tactical operation to Lt. Thomas Weaver of the *Cabot*. Nathan Miller, *Sea of Glory; the Continental Navy Fights for Independence, 1775–1783* (New York: David McKay Co., 1974), pp. 107–9. Jones described the action in a letter to Joseph Hewes, April 14, 1776. Jones Papers, Library of Congress (hereafter cited as Jones Papers); and William Bell Clark et al., eds., *Naval Documents of the American Revolution* (Washington: Department of the Navy, 1964–), 4:815–18. Esek Hopkins, commander of the American fleet, sent his official account of the expedition to John Hancock on April 8, 1776, but it does not mention Jones. Esek Hopkins, *The Letter Book of Esek Hopkins, Commander-in-Chief of the United States Navy, 1775–1777*, ed. Alverda S. Beck (Providence: Printed for the Rhode Island Historical Society, 1932), pp. 46–48. Other informative documents are in Clark, *Naval Documents*, 4:152–53, 173–76.

[4] This action occurred in the Block Island Channel, where HMS *Rose* and several smaller vessels had been ordered by Admiral Graves to bottle up Rhode Island privateers. The bomb brig *Bolton* and the armed tender *Hawk*, part of this force, were the vessels Jones alludes to here. See Jones to Hewes, April 14, 1776, Jones Papers. Supporting documents, including extracts from the journal of HMS *Glasgow* and a report from its captain, Tyringham Howe, are in Clark, *Naval Documents*, 4:679–82.

[5] Jones reported that the *Alfred* lost five men killed and seven wounded. John Paul Jones, "Memorandum of the Engagement With the Glasgow," and Jones to Joseph Hewes, May 19, 1776, Jones Papers.

Island. A council of war having dismissed the captain of the *Providence*,[6] one of the ships of the squadron, Mr. Hopkins gave me written orders to take command of her and to escort some troops that were going from Rhode Island to New York to serve under the orders of General Washington. I soon completed this mission and, having refitted my ship for duty within a few days, I was ordered to escort from Rhode Island a heavy artillery train destined for the defense of New York. I then experienced great difficulty from two enemy frigates that were charged with preventing communications between the two places. I had two separate engagements with one of them, the *Cerberus* of 32 guns—the first to protect my convoy and the second to shelter a vessel from St. Domingue, richly laden with munitions and stores for Congress.

Then I received orders to return to Boston to provide an escort for a number of public ships headed for Philadelphia. While executing this commission I had several encounters with warships destined for New York under the command of Lord Howe; however, I was able to preserve my convoy and I arrived in the Delaware on August 1, 1776.[7]

On the eighth of the same month the president of Congress personally presented a commission to me as captain in the U. S. Navy. It was the first that the Congress had granted since the Declaration of *Independence* on the preceding fourth of July.[8]

Congress had ordered the construction of 13 frigates, but because none of them was ready, I was ordered to put to sea

---

[6] Jones replaced John Hazard as commander of the *Providence* on May 10 and at the same time received orders to transport the men, who had enlisted in the navy from the Continental army, to New York City. Esek Hopkins to Jones, May 10, 1776, Papers of the Continental Congress, National Archives and Records Service (hereafter cited as PCC), item 58, fol. 149. See also Jones to Joseph Hewes, May 19, 1776, Jones Papers. Both items are in Clark, *Naval Documents*, 5:27, 151–53.

[7] Hopkins first ordered Jones to proceed to Newburyport, Mass., and from there to convoy several ships loaded with coal to Philadelphia, but he later redirected Jones to Boston. Jones arrived in the Delaware River early in August, after convoying the schooner *First Attempt* from Boston to Egg Harbor, N. J. Esek Hopkins to Jones, June 13 and 18, 1776, PCC, item 58, fols. 155, 157; Jones to John Hancock, July 30, 1776. All are in Clark, *Naval Documents*, 5:509, 599, 1286.

[8] Jones' claim is misleading because Congress also issued at least one other captain's commission on August 8, 1776. Clark, *Naval Documents*, 6:125. Furthermore, on October 10, 1776, when Congress sought to bring order to the naval officers' claims of seniority, Jones was ranked 18th in a list of 24. Worthington C. Ford, ed., *Journals of the Continental Congress, 1774–1789*, 34 vols. (Washington; Library of Congress, 1904–37), 6:861. Hereafter cited as *JCC*.

alone and to engage the enemy in the manner I judged most favorable to the interests of the *United States*.[9] The *Providence* was a lightly armed ship carrying only 70 men and 12 small cannon.

Near the Bermuda Islands I encountered the frigate *Solebay* of 32 guns with a convoy. She was part of Admiral Parker's squadron which had been defeated and driven from Charleston; she was bound for New York. I wanted to avoid an engagement with such a superior force but my officers and crew stubbornly insisted that it was the fleet from Jamaica, and as it was necessary at this point in the war to command by persuasion, the result was a serious engagement lasting six hours, which at the end was carried out at pistol range. An audacious maneuver being my only recourse, I tried it with success and disengaged myself.

Soon thereafter I took some important prizes and afterward sailed toward the coast of Acadia to destroy the whale and cod fisheries there.

Near Sable Island I encountered the *Milford*, an enemy frigate of 32 guns, with which it was impossible to avoid an engagement. We cannonaded each other from 10 o'clock in the morning until sunset, but the battle was neither as close nor as hot as that with the *Solebay*. At length I disengaged by passing the flats of the island, and the next day I entered the port of Canso where I did indeed destroy fisheries and shipping.

The morning of the following day I set sail for Isle de *Madame* where I made two raids, destroying the fisheries and burning all of the vessels that I could not carry away. This expedition took place during stormy weather and on a dangerous coast, heavily populated with residents and in a ready state of defense, but I had the good fortune to succeed despite all of these obstacles.

From there I sailed to Rhode Island, where I arrived six weeks and five days after my departure from the Delaware.

---

[9] On August 6 the Marine Committee ordered Jones "to proceed immediately on a Cruize against our Enemies. We think in & about the Lattitude of Bermuda may prove the most favourable ground for your purpose." Marine Committee to Jones, August 6, 1776, PCC, item 58, fols. 161–62. Jones had claimed in 1776 that "it was proposed to Send me from Philadelphia by Land to take Command of the *Hampden* in Connecticut, but I rather preferred to continue in the *Providence*, the *Hampden* being a far inferiour Vessel to the description that had been given of her to Congress." Jones to John Hancock, December 7, 1776, Jones Papers.

During that time I had taken 16 prizes, not counting the vessels that were destroyed.[10]

The commander in chief, who had not put to sea since the expedition of the *Providence*, then adopted a plan which I had proposed to him. This was, first, to destroy the enemy's coal vessels and fisheries at Isle Royale. Second, to release more than 300 American citizens who were imprisoned in the coal mines. Three vessels were designated for this service, the *Alfred*, the *Hampden*, and the *Providence*; but the *Hampden*, damaged when grounding on a rock, could not accompany me. On November 2, 1776, I continued on my route with the *Alfred*, which I commanded, accompanied only by the *Providence*. Off the coast of Acadia I captured a vessel from Liverpool and immediately after, on the latitude of Louisbourg, I took the *Mellish*, a large armed vessel, having on board two English naval officers and an army captain with a company of soldiers. The *Mellish* was carrying 2,000 complete sets of uniforms to Canada for the army posted there under the command of Generals Carleton and Burgoyne.

The *Providence* then became separated from the *Alfred* during the night for no reason whatsoever. I was left alone, and during the bad season, on the enemy coast; but despite being embarrassed by my prizes and prisoners, I did not want to abandon my project. I made one raid on the coast of Acadia and burned a transport vessel of great value that the enemy had run aground on the beach. I also burned the warehouses and some whaling and codfishing vessels; there was a great quantity of oil consumed, too, with the warehouses.

I then captured, near Isle Royale, three transports and a fourth transport loaded with codfish and furs. I learned from one of these ships that the harbors of Isle Royale were closed by ice, which made the expedition I was planning impractical. These prizes had been escorted by the frigate *Flora*, then close by but hidden from view by fog. The next day I captured a *privateer* from Liverpool carrying 16 cannon; I then made sail to bring my prizes to some United States port.

---

[10] Jones' contemporary reports listed eight prizes that were sent to port and eight ships that were sunk, burnt, or destroyed. Jones to the Marine Committee, September 30, 1776, PCC, item 58, fols. 89–94. Additional details of this voyage are provided in Jones' letters to the Marine Committee and to Robert Morris, which are in Clark, *Naval Documents*, 6:684–87, 745, 1047–50, 1302–4, 1457–58.

At the latitude of Boston I again encountered the frigate *Milford*. The *Alfred*, which by then carried a greatly reduced crew and many prisoners, was very inferior in strength; I would have preferred to avoid an engagement that did not promise any advantage, but my prizes—chiefly the *Mellish*—obliged me to take that risk, no matter what the chances of success. At nightfall, therefore, I placed myself between my prizes and the enemy and, having given the necessary instructions to the prizes as to how to avoid all danger and to arrive at some safe port, I changed my course during the night, set out a ship's lantern, and in this way drew the enemy into pursuing me. This stratagem saved my prizes. The next day I was fortunate to escape after a serious action with the *Milford* that was not interrupted or terminated until evening and then by a hard gale. I arrived at Boston on December 16, 1776, having only enough water and provisions for two days; my prizes arrived safely except for one of the smaller ones that the enemy recaptured.[11]

The news of the uniforms captured aboard the *Mellish* renewed the courage of General Washington's army, which at that time was nearly destitute of clothing. This unexpected relief contributed not insignificantly to the success of the army at the battle of Trenton (against the Hessians) that occurred immediately after my arrival in Boston.[12]

I paid the wages due to the crews of the *Alfred* and the *Providence* out of my own purse and lent the remainder of my money to Congress. That honorable assembly, on February 5, sent orders from Philadelphia for me to command and conduct a secret expedition that was important in several respects. Its principal goal was to levy contributions on the island of St. Christopher and on the northern side of Jamaica, then to

---

[11] Jones' contemporary letters support this later account of his destructive voyage to Cape Breton. Jones to Esek Hopkins, November 2, 1776; Jones to the Marine Committee, November 12 and 16, 1776, and January 12, 1777, PCC, item 58, fols. 97, 99, 101, 107–11; "Notes of the Time of Material Occurences During the *Alfred*'s Cruise in Novr. & Decr. 1776," December 10, 1776, Jones Papers.

[12] Morison in *Jones*, p. 80, accepts Jones' suggestion that some of the clothing reached Washington's army before Trenton. However, George Washington refers to the capture of the clothes on December 12, 1776, and their future distribution on January 24, 1777. Washington to the president of Congress, December 12, 1776, Washington to Jonathan Trumbull, January 24, 1777, in George Washington, *The Writings of George Washington*, ed. John C. Fitzpatrick, 39 vols. (Washington: U. S. Government Printing Office, 1931–44), 6:356, 7:58.

attack and seize Pensacola. The small squadron designated for this expedition was composed of the *Alfred*, the *Columbus*, the *Cabot*, the *Hampden*, and the *Providence*. The project was conceived by me, and I had discussed it with Mr. Morris, who later was minister of finance; but the jealousy of Mr. Hopkins, the commander in chief, so compromised this enterprise that it did not occur.[13] Wishing then to render an account of these events to Congress in person, I left Boston for Philadelphia by land. Mr. Hopkins was first suspended and soon after was dismissed from the service.[14] The season was so advanced that the expedition was abandoned and Congress resolved to give me command of the frigate *Comte D'Argout*, while awaiting an occasion to employ me to better advantage. But before I had time to exercise that command, the Secret Committee of Congress ordered me to embark with my officers and sailors on *l'Amphitrite*, a French ship destined to leave Portsmouth (in New Hampshire) for France, and from there we were to proceed to Holland in order to take command of *l'Indienne*, an extraordinary frigate carrying 36-pound cannon and constructed in Holland for Congress. However, since the commanding officer of *l'Amphitrite* did not accept the proposition, Congress instructed me to outfit the *Ranger*, a frigate of 18 guns, with orders to use this small vessel to go take command of *l'Indienne* and to keep the *Ranger* as my escort. This last frigate was not yet fully armed, but when General Burgoyne and his army were forced to surrender at Saratoga, it was I who carried this interesting news to Nantes, where I arrived December 2, 1777.[15] During my passage I took two prizes from a convoy coming from the Mediterranean under the protection of the *Invincible*

---

[13] For further details of this proposed expedition, see Jones to Robert Morris, January 12, 1777, and the Marine Committee to Jones, February 1, 1777, Jones Papers; and Robert Morris to Jones, February 5, 1777, PCC, item 168, fols. 5–9.

[14] Jones, an earlier supporter of Hopkins, was only one of his accusers. But Congress' disappointment with the navy's inactivity was probably the key to why Hopkins was suspended on March 26, 1777, and on January 2, 1778, was "dismissed from the service of the United States." JCC, 7:202, 204, 10:13. Depositions against Hopkins are in PCC, item 58, fols. 224–38. Lorenz, *Jones*, pp. 105–9; Jones to Hewes, April 14, 1776, and Jones to Robert Morris, April 7, 1777, Jones Papers.

[15] Morison says that although the *Ranger* was the bearer of duplicate dispatches from Congress to Benjamin Franklin announcing this victory, the French merchantman *Penet*, carrying the original dispatches, beat her across the Atlantic. Morison, *Jones*, p. 111.

of 74 guns. For an entire day, in fair weather, I sailed very close to this ship and I captured the two prizes under its cannon.[16]

During January 1778, I journeyed from Nantes to Paris to make arrangements with the American ministers for equipping *l'Indienne*. But because the news of General Burgoyne's capture had by then determined the French court to recognize the independence of America by a treaty of alliance, and because the English ambassador at The Hague had discovered (by obtaining possession of the papers of an American minister) that *l'Indienne* belonged to Congress, I acquiesced in the wishes of the American ministers, and it was decided that the most prudent way to preserve this frigate until Congress could take effective measures to employ it in the American service was to cede it to His Most Christian Majesty.

This being done, I returned to my little frigate, the *Ranger*, which was at Nantes. On February 10, 1778, I received from America some information relative to the stations and force of the warships and frigates that were in America under the command of Lord Howe. I wrote the same day to Mr. Deane, one of the American ministers at Paris, giving him a detailed plan for an expedition to be attempted in America, with a squadron of only 10 ships of the line and some frigates and troops, in order to destroy once and for all time the power of the English in the United States before reinforcements could be sent from England.

France then had in its Atlantic ports 30 ships of the line and many frigates equipped and ready for service. Never before had she had, and perhaps never again would she have, a better chance to strike such a decisive blow against the English navy. If this plan had been adopted without delay and if a squadron had been detached immediately from Brest to execute it, Great Britain would have had no knowledge of this devastating project until its effects had been consummated in America. Lord Howe would have been surprised and taken prisoner in the Delaware. Americans could then immediately have manned his fleet and, sending small detachments right and left, they could easily have annihilated the English naval forces on the American coasts

---

[16] For additional daily details on the voyages of the *Ranger*, November 1, 1777, to September 27, 1778, see the diary of the frigate's surgeon, "Diary of Dr. Ezra Green," *New England Historical and Genealogical Register* 29 (1875): 13–24.

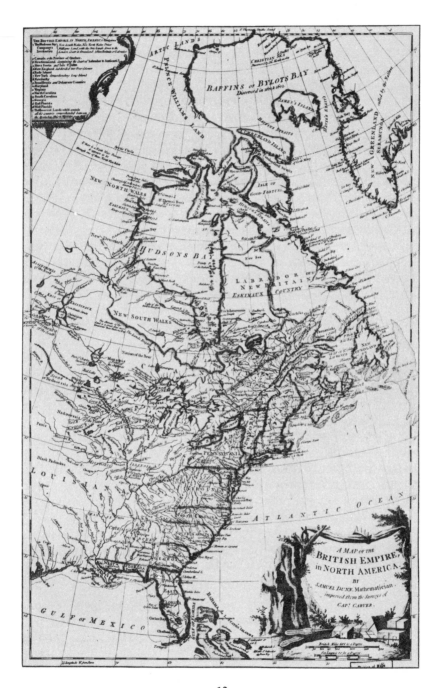

13

before the arrival of Admiral Byron. American enthusiasm would certainly then have so strengthened Washington that he could have taken New York and destroyed or captured all English troops in the *United States*. At the same time, the French squadron, entering New York harbor under English colors, could have trapped and captured Lord Byron and successively all the vessels of his fleet, as one after the other the ships—dispersed by storms during the crossing—arrived in port. Thus in one campaign, and with little expense, France would have had an excellent chance to establish American independence and strike a blow that would have brought Great Britain to her knees, forcing her to recognize she was no longer mistress of the ocean. What will posterity think of France's having neglected this inestimable opportunity? Will it not be clear that the original error was only compounded by adopting the plan three months after, when it was too late, and by sending the French fleet from Toulon rather than that from Brest, at the cost of yet another month? It is useless to describe in detail the unfortunate consequences of this delay, but the general result was a long, bloody, expensive war that eventually involved France, Holland, Spain, and the East Indies.[17]

When Mr. Deane informed the court at Versailles of my plan for the expedition to America, he showed such bad faith as to take credit for this project and call himself the author; as a result, he received a portrait of His Majesty on a gold box set with diamonds.

In the meantime, I escorted several American vessels leaving Nantes for Quiberon Bay, where M. de la Motte-Piquet waited with five ships of the line and some frigates under orders to protect and escort them until they were west of Cape Finisterre. The departure of M. de la Motte-Piquet caused no alarm in England, though his destination was unknown.

I reached Quiberon Bay on February 13, 1778. I asked M. de la Motte-Piquet *if he would return my salute;* that brave officer agreed to do so. Neither he nor I knew that the alliance

---

[17] The Toulon fleet under the comte d'Estaing departed on April 18, 1778, but when it reached the Delaware on July 8 Lord Howe had already concentrated his forces in New York. The disappointing and indecisive Rhode Island campaign followed. Morison, *Jones*, p. 127. Ira D. Gruber, *The Howe Brothers and the American Revolution* (New York: Published for the Institute of Early American History and Culture at Williamsburg, Va., by Atheneum, 1972), pp. 304–24.

between France and America had been signed seven days before at Versailles. This was the first salute received by the American flag from any sovereign power and gave birth to much dispute in the Parliament of England.[18]

I went immediately from Quiberon Bay to Brest; I did not enter the roads, but I dropped anchor at Cameret. There I was detained by contrary winds until the ambassador of France announced at London the final treaty between His Most Christian Majesty and the *United States*. Then I entered the roads of Brest and saluted the comte d'Orvilliers, who returned the salute and received me with the honors due an admiral on board his flagship, *la Bretagne*. On arriving at Cameret, I communicated to the comte d'Orvilliers my plan for an expedition to America. This commander strongly approved it and immediately sent a copy to M. de Sartine.

In the month of February 1776 the English Parliament had passed a law authorizing George III to treat all Americans captured in arms at sea as "*traitors, pirates* and *felons*." This circumstance more than any other made me the declared enemy of Great Britain. Never before had history furnished an example of a people so arrogant as to claim sovereignty of the seas! Never before had it revealed premeditated cruelty such as that which anticipates the crime. From the beginning of the war in America the exchange of prisoners from the ground forces had been arranged between General Washington and the English generals. Despite all her pride Great Britain had been obliged to respect these arrangements and to consider as prisoners of war all the Americans who were captured *while in the army;* but it was not the same for service at sea. To be taken with arms in hand against England on her pretended empire of the ocean was an unforgivable crime according to the published annals of her Parliament. If at the time of this act of Parliament the strength of the English navy had been compared with that of the

---

[18] This was probably not the first salute to the American flag, because the American privateer *General Mifflin* had received a nine-gun salute in 1777. Gardner Allen speculates that the French admiral "had received some intimation of the propriety of returning an American salute" when the incident occurred. William Carmichael, Silas Deane's secretary, advised Jones to accept a nine-gun rather than an 11-gun salute. However, Jones complained to the Marine Committee on February 22, 1778, that he was offered only a nine-gun answer. The French admiral said this was the return "authorized by his court" for "Holland or any other Republic." Gardner W. Allen, *A Naval History of the American Revolution*, 2 vols. (Boston: Houghton Mifflin Co., 1913), 1:339–40; Morison, *Jones*, pp. 128–30. Jones to the Marine Committee, February 22, 1778, PCC, item 58, fols. 143–45.

American navy, a relationship of a hundred to one would have been found. Noble sons of liberty, may this be the basis of your glorious renown. May your enemies remember forever how their cruelties were exercised in vain! That far from abating your courage, they forced you, with your tremendous acts of heroism, to sustain the American flag on the oceans that the author of nature created free. Cruelty and fear have always been companions. Only fear has prevented England from giving to the world, for a second time on the occasion of this war, the revolting spectacle of the horrors that ravaged Scotland in 1745. How great would have been the satisfaction of this people, as ferocious as they are vindictive, if they could have hanged until half dead the Americans *captured at sea*, then cut open their breasts with a knife, and thrown their beating hearts into the flames! If they did not dare attempt this, they did throw a number of American citizens into English prisons where they were kept for five full years, suffered from cold, hunger, and beating, and endured all kinds of outrages. Some of these unfortunate men were sold on the coast of Africa and others were transported to India. The firmness with which these patriot martyrs sustained all these reverses is unexampled. They preferred persecution to saving themselves by serving in the English navy.[19]

Justly indignant at the treatment meted out to these Americans, I resolved to make a great effort to procure their relief and to bring to an end the barbarous ravages perpetrated by the English in America, burning homes, destroying property and even entire towns. I received no orders to secure reparations for these misfortunes and I had not communicated my plan to this end to the American ministers residing in Paris. I proposed to descend on some part of England and there destroy merchant shipping. My plan was also to take someone of particular distinction as a prisoner and to hold him as hostage to guarantee the lives and exchange of Americans then imprisoned in England. M. d'Orvilliers, to whom I communicated this project,

---

[19] For more information on American sailors in English prisons, including the prison activities of Henry and Cutting Lunt, who later became officers on the *Bonhomme Richard*, see Samuel Cutler, "Prison Ships, and the 'Old Mill Prison,' Plymouth England, 1777, Journal of Samuel Cutler," *New England Historical and Genealogical Register* 32 (1878): 42–44, 184–88, 305–8, 395–98; and Jeremiah Colburn, "A List of the Americans Committed to Old Mill Prison Since the American War, 1776–1782," *New England Historical and Genealogical Register* 19 (1865): 74–76, 136–41, 209–13.

offered to procure a captain's commission in the royal navy for me so that in case I ran into superior forces I could claim the protection of France, not yet at war with England; but despite the advantages that this offer held for me, I felt it was necessary to refuse because I had not been authorized by Congress to change my flag and because had I accepted such a commission from France my devotion to the cause of America might have been doubted.

I sailed from Brest and advanced toward the Irish Sea, passing within striking distance of a number of vessels I could have captured, but I did not want to risk dispersing my crew. By the 17th of April everything was prepared for a raid on England, but strong, contrary winds forced me to sail on to the coast of Ireland. Near the entrance into *Carrack-fergus* I seized a fishing boat carrying six men who turned out to be pilots. The *Drake*, an English frigate of 20 guns, was then in the roads of *Carrack-fergus* and within view. I thought it would be possible to seize her at night by surprise.[20] To this end, I made the necessary preparations and forced the pilots to guide the *Ranger* to the enemy. But the mate, who had drunk too much brandy, did not drop the anchor at the instant the order was given to him, and that prevented the *Ranger* from running alongside the *Drake* as I had planned. I believed that since my entrance into the roads had not given an alarm, the most prudent action was to cut my cable and return immediately to the channel. Battered by a storm, I remained there three days and, the weather becoming more favorable, I attempted a second time to descend on England. This plan greatly alarmed the lieutenants on the *Ranger:* "Their object," they said, "was *gain not honor.*" They were poor: instead of encouraging the morale of the crew, they excited them to disobedience; they persuaded them that they had the right to judge whether a measure that was proposed to them was good or bad.[21]

---

[20] The *Ranger's* surgeon, Ezra Green, noted that Jones had wanted "to go in and cut her out" when the *Drake* was first sighted, "but the wind blowing fresh and the people unwilling to undertake it we stood off and on till midnight . . . ." "Diary of Dr. Ezra Green," p. 18.

[21] For Jones' contemporary assessment of the raid on Whitehaven and the capture of the *Drake*, see Jones to the U.S. commissioners, May 27, 1778; Jones to Edward Bancroft, August 14, 1778; and Jones to the U.S. commissioners, August 15, 1778; all in the Jones Papers. For other contemporary American and British accounts, see Allen, *Naval History*, 1:337–54. Although there are some minor variations in details, the major elements of Jones' testimony remain unchallenged.

I was within sight of Whitehaven, a rather shallow port which contained approximately 400 foreign and domestic merchantmen, averaging 250-tons burden each. My plan was to take advantage of the ebb tide: the ships would then be aground and keeled over. To carry out this project, it was necessary for me to land about midnight with a party of determined volunteers and to seize first the fort and then a battery of heavy cannon that defended the port. My two lieutenants, not demonstrating the high spirit this enterprise required and not wanting to reveal their true motive, declared they were ill with fatigue.[22] I resolved to provide the example and to command the attack in person. Only with much effort and loss of time did I engage 30 volunteers to accompany me. With this handful of men and two small boats, I left the *Ranger* at 11 o'clock at night and rowed toward Whitehaven, but the distance to shore proved to be greater than I had judged, and with the tide against us dawn broke before we had effected a landing. I sent the smaller boat to the north side of the port to set fire to the merchantmen while I advanced with the other to the south side to take possession of the fort and battery. The fort was taken by assault; we did not use scaling ladders but climbed on the shoulders of the biggest and most robust men and by this means we entered the fort through its embrasures. As I was the commander of this operation, I was also the first to enter the fort. The morning was cold and the sentinels had retired into their guardhouses, not expecting an enemy visit. As I secured their entrance, there was no bloodshed. The fort's 36-gun battery was spiked, and I advanced toward the southern part of the port to burn the ships there, when to my great astonishment I saw that the boat sent to the north had returned and had not accomplished anything. Those who manned it pretended to have been intimidated by certain noises they had heard, but I told them that *the noise existed only in their imagination.* Believing, however, that it was too late to send them back toward the northern sector, I assembled my small forces and

---

[22] The accounts of David Freeman, a deserter from the *Ranger*, and W. Brownrigg and Henry Ellison, justices of the peace at Whitehaven, differ slightly from that of Jones. They reported that about 200 ships were in the harbor and only one ship was burned during the raid. If anything, Jones underestimated the confusion and concern that he left in his wake. See letters and testimony related to the Whitehaven raid in the Public Record Office, State Papers Domestic, George III, vol. 12.

tried to set fires in the south, hoping they would soon spread everywhere. In fact, the fires did spread and rose to a great height. But because it was nearly 8 o'clock in the morning and because thousands of inhabitants began to gather, I could no longer postpone my retreat. I made it in very good order. When all of my force was embarked I remained for several minutes on the far breakwater to contemplate at length the terror, panic, and stupidity of the inhabitants, who numbered no less than 10,000 and stood as still as statues or scurried senselessly here and there to gain some high ground beyond the city. The oarsmen had already rowed some distance from shore before the English risked approaching their fort, and when they found their cannon spiked they brought some pieces from vessels and fired toward our dinghies. I responded to their salute by firing mortars that I had placed in the stern of my boat.

Once back on board the *Ranger*, and the wind being favorable, I made sail for the coast of Scotland. My intention was to seize Count Selkirk and detain him as a hostage in conformity with the plan of which I have already spoken. For this purpose, I landed on the lord's estate about noon of the same day with only two officers and a small guard in one boat. Upon landing I met some inhabitants who, taking me for an Englishman, told me that Lord Selkirk was in London, but that his wife and several ladies of her acquaintance were in the castle. This made me resolve to go at once to the boat in order to return to the *Ranger*. This moderate conduct did not suit my men, who were disposed to pillage, burn, and plunder all they could. Even though that would have been to wage war in the manner of the English, I did not believe in imitating them, particularly on this occasion when I considered the respects due to a lady. It was necessary, however, to find a way to satisfy the cupidity of my crew and at the same time spare Lady Selkirk. I had only an instant to think of a way: what seemed to me the most proper for all concerned was to order the two officers[23] to repair to the castle with the guard, which was to remain outside under arms while the officers entered alone. They could then politely demand the family plate, stopping for only a few minutes and accepting what was given them without further

---

[23] David Cullam and Samuel Wallingford.

inquiry, returning without further search. I was punctually obeyed and the plate was delivered. Lady Selkirk herself commented several times to the officers that she was very touched by the moderation I had shown. She even wanted to come to the shore—more than a mile distant from her castle—to invite me to dine with her, but the officers requested her not to quit her home.

The next day, April 24, 1778, I was back in the roads of Carrack-fergus where, as I have already said, the *Drake*, an English frigate of 20 guns, was at anchor. My intention was to enter the roads and attack this frigate in broad daylight, but in the eyes of the lieutenants the project was by no means right because it involved honor more than self-interest, their only motive. The crew of the *Ranger* took this occasion to mutiny so that I ran the risk of being killed or thrown overboard.[24] Two days earlier I had nearly been abandoned on the shore at Whitehaven. In the meantime the captain of the *Drake*,[25] having been informed of our landing at Whitehaven, prepared to sail. His boat was sent out with an officer and a telescope to reconnoiter the *Ranger*. I took advantage of this occasion to disguise my ship. I masked my guns and had my crew remain out of sight. The *Ranger* having the air of a merchantman, the boat from the *Drake* was deceived, drew alongside, and was captured. This trifling success had such an exhilarating effect on my crew that they no longer objected to giving battle. The *Drake*, having fired several cannon in a vain attempt to recall her boat, hoisted anchor to come out and engage the *Ranger*. The *Drake*, filled with volunteers, had two more cannon than the *Ranger* and nearly double the manpower. It was accompanied by a number of small yachts that had gentlemen and ladies on board as if for a pleasant outing. The *Ranger* awaited the approach of the *Drake* and allowed it to cross half the channel, which separated Scotland and Ireland, before commencing the battle. When the affair became serious and it was evident that the *Ranger* would not withdraw, the yachts immediately

---

[24] Dr. Green's diary entry for April 24 supports Jones' account. "Early in the morning our Capt. proposed making a second attempt to cut out the Ship in Caracfergus, which was now within a small Distance, the People both officers & men discovr'd great unwillingness to make the attempt." "Diary of Dr. Ezra Green," p. 20.

[25] Capt. George Burdon commanded the *Drake*. Lorenz, *Jones*, p. 171; Jones to the U.S. commissioners, August 15, 1778, Jones Papers.

retired to a respectful distance and then decided it would be prudent to retreat.

I did not start engaging the enemy until they were within pistol range. At this distance a lively action was sustained for an hour and five minutes, after which the English frigate lowered her flag. Her captain had just been wounded in the head by a musket ball, from which he died. The lieutenant, also mortally wounded, survived only two days. I regretted that these brave men had to perish and I buried them at sea with the honors they deserved. The six honest fishermen, whom I mentioned before, had lost their boat sunk in the sea during the bad weather that preceded the descent on Whitehaven. I was fortunate enough to find in my own purse sufficient English gold to replace their loss and recompense their services. The *Drake* was heavily damaged in her masts and rigging; she lost 42 men either killed or wounded during the action. I had taken several other prizes, but because I had left France with only 123 men I could man only two of these prizes, which arrived safely at Brest; the others were burned or sunk.

With the *Ranger*, the *Drake*, and one other prize I ran westward of Ireland and arrived at Brest on May 7, having been absent only 28 days and having taken more than 200 prisoners.

This expedition caused great harm to Great Britain and she found it necessary not only to fortify her ports but also to arm the Volunteers of Ireland. This was later substantiated by Lord Mountmorris in a public speech.[26]

When circumstances had obliged me to permit my men to demand Lady Selkirk's family plate, I had resolved to redeem it with my own funds whenever it should be sold and return it to the lady. Consequently, when we arrived in Brest my first task was to write her a moving letter, in which I described the motives for my expedition and the cruel necessity I was under to inflict punishment in retaliation for English conduct in America.[27] This letter was sent by packet to the postmaster

---

[26] Jones' raid and the capture of the *Drake* reportedly caused widespread alarm on the west coast of Britain. *The London Chronicle*, April 24–28, 28–30, April 30–May 2, and May 2–5, 1778. For Jones' activities as reported in English newspapers see Don C. Seitz, *Paul Jones, His Exploits During 1778–1780* (New York: E. P. Dutton and Co., 1917), pp. 3–25.

[27] Jones to the countess of Selkirk, May 8, 1778, Jones Papers. A copy with a copy of the cover letter to Benjamin Franklin is in PCC, item 168, 1:73–78. See the documentary evidence section of this memoir, Jones to Lady Selkirk, November 8, 1784.

general in London, so that it could be shown to the English king and his ministers, and so the court at London would be forced to renounce the bloody act of Parliament and exchange those American *"traitors, pirates, and felons"* for the prisoners of war I had captured and sent to France.

The comte d'Orvilliers sent a detailed account of my expedition to the minister of marine, who wrote to Dr. Franklin that His Majesty wanted me to come to Versailles: "That the king wanted to employ me as commander of secret expeditions and that to this end he would give me *l'Indienne* and other frigates with troops in order to undertake landings, etc." As a result Dr. Franklin wrote to me informing me of the project and instructing me to keep it a secret between us, as the government had not seen fit to inform even the other American ministers in Paris of it.[28]

M. de Sartine received me with much distinction and made me the most flattering promises. The prince of Nassau was sent to Holland to make the necessary arrangements to equip and arm *l'Indienne*. But before anything relative to the project for which I had been called could be effected, war began between France and England with the engagement of *la Belle-Poule*. This embarrassed the minister of marine and the difficulty was not lessened by the news which the prince of Nassau reported upon his return from Holland—that the Dutch were opposed to the outfitting of *l'Indienne*. I offered to return to the *Ranger*, but in order to persuade me to stay M. de Sartine had written an officious letter to the three American ministers and obtained their formal consent for me to remain in Europe and execute any assignment I might receive. As the main fleet had been ordered at that moment to put to sea from Brest, and because no measures to employ me were forthcoming, I offered to embark with the comte d'Orvilliers. The minister answered that the king appreciated this offer, but he could not consent

---

[28] Benjamin Franklin asked Jones to consider an expedition against the "Jersey privateers." A few days later, Franklin informed Jones that the prince of Nassau would go to Holland to bring back a powerful frigate under the guise of a French merchantman. "The other commissioners are not acquainted with this proposition as yet, as you see, by the nature of it, that it is necessary to be kept a secret till we have got the vessel here, for fear of difficulties in Holland and interruption." Franklin to Jones, May 27, June 1, 1778. Francis Wharton, ed., *The Revolutionary Diplomatic Correspondence of the United States*, 6 vols. (Washington: U.S. Government Printing Office, 1889), 2:599–600.

because it was his intention to provide more useful employment for me during this interval.

Thereupon I was requested to send my ideas for employing a small, light squadron destined for secret missions to the minister. I seized the opportunity and proposed several plans on that subject: among others, to destroy the power of England in Africa and in Hudson Bay; to destroy the Newfoundland fisheries; to intercept the English fleets from the East and West Indies; and, what was then more important, to intercept the Baltic fleet, which was escorted by only one frigate. I had received personal information from England concerning this last project, and I offered to undertake it with only three frigates and three *cutters*. The minister adopted this plan, and I came to Brest to take command of one of the frigates which were then stationed in that port and to take under my overall command two other frigates with the cutters that were at St. Malo. When I arrived at Brest, the comte d'Orvilliers had given the command of the frigate in question to a French officer. Because there was not a moment to lose, the senior officer of the frigates stationed at St. Malo was dispatched against the Baltic fleet, but since he did not approach close enough to the English coast, he was unable to accomplish his mission and returned to Brest.

At the same time the minister sent orders to the comte d'Orvilliers to receive me on board *la Bretagne*, but the comte had already left Brest for the second time before receiving this dispatch. M. de la Prevally, who commanded at Brest and had a rather bad disposition, did not permit me to embark on the frigate that carried dispatches to the main fleet.

So I remained at Brest in this most disagreeable situation, not being at liberty to say on what grounds I had left the *Ranger*.[29] I was the object of much jealousy and false speculation among the naval officers.

From the beginning of my relationship with the comte d'Orvilliers I was treated with special distinction and I received several important lessons on naval tactics and on the details of conducting fleets and their operations.

---

[29] For Jones' frustrated plans and inactivity during the summer and fall of 1778, see Jones to the commissioners at Paris, August 15, 1778; Benjamin Franklin to Jones, September 6, 1778, July 8, 1779; Franklin and John Adams to Jones, February 10, 1779; Franklin's instructions to Jones, April 28, 1779. Wharton, *Diplomatic Correspondence*, 2:683–84, 703; 3:42, 145–46, 242.

After many plans had miscarried and much time had been lost because of the indecision of the minister of marine, he invited me at the beginning of December 1778 to go from Brest to Lorient to examine some Compagnie des Indes vessels that were then for sale. I found that some of them could be converted to warships, above all *le Maréchal de Broglio*, a new ship capable of mounting 64 guns. The minister, however, did not take any decisive action, but allowed two more months to pass without deciding anything.

Because I had already lost nine months since agreeing to remain in Europe under the orders of the court and as I did not see an end to my disagreeable situation, I went by stage to Versailles, determined to return to America if the minister did not immediately give me a command. When I left Lorient I recalled the words of Poor Richard: "If you want your affairs to prosper, go yourself; if not, send someone." This led me to say to myself that if the minister gave me satisfaction, I would call the ship that I personally commanded the *Bonhomme Richard*.

The minister of marine received me very well and apologized to me for the past. He urged me to accept command of *le Maréchal de Broglio*, to which he proposed to add three or four frigates and two fireships, and he promised to embark 500 men from the Régiment de Walsh Irlandais as landing troops.[30] But despairing of finding in Europe a sufficient number of American sailors to man *le Maréchal de Broglio*, I was obliged to refuse the command of that beautiful vessel; and because the minister again promised me *l'Indienne*, I temporarily accepted *le Duras*, which I called the *Bonhomme Richard*, a small vessel that, having made four voyages to India, was very old and in bad condition.[31]

M. Garnier, who had been chargé d'affaires in England, a man of great insight and sound judgment, helped me make all the arrangements with the minister concerning the small squadron I was destined to command. I had adopted, in agreement with

---

[30] The "Régiment de Walsh Irlandais," or Régiment de Walsh-Serrant, was an Irish force of marine infantry commanded by François Jacques, vicomte de Walsh-Serrant. Walsh-Serrant to Jones, June 14, 1779, Jones Papers; Bibliothèque du service historique de l'armée, Corps des troupes; Infanterie de Walsh-Serrant, fols. 1–104.

[31] The vessel *Duc de Duras*, which Jones renamed the *Bonhomme Richard*, or *Poor Richard*, was built in 1766. Jones decided she was "the only Ship offered for sale in France that will answer our purpose." Morison, *Jones*, p. 182.

him, several plans related to different important operations I wanted to undertake, having carte blanche. It was the most irritating of misfortunes that I was deprived of the aid of a man of such ability almost immediately after that. M. Garnier was destined to succeed M. Gérard as the king's minister in America; a very different man was his successor.[32] In my opinion this commissioner was lacking in judgment, uncertain, and indiscreet. He was consistent only in the things that affected his interests, so that the minister made an error in judgment when he confided public affairs to such a man.

As the proper cannon could not be found at Lorient to arm the *Bonhomme Richard*, I went to Bordeaux and from there to Angoulême, where I contracted for the cannon which were needed. On my return to Lorient, I enlisted 30 American sailors who had just arrived from England, where they had been exchanged. At Nantes I found an express letter from the court. The marquis de Lafayette had come from America to France and wanted to join me for an expedition, and he had obtained from the king the command of troops for this purpose.[33] As a result, I was ordered to return immediately to the court to make the necessary arrangements. The commissioner was ignorant of the terms that had been agreed to between M. Garnier and myself, wherein, as I previously noted, I had carte blanche and was the sole commander. The affair then took on a new aspect. I was not reluctant to share my authority with the marquis de Lafayette; I was certain that the two of us could act in concert and with mutual confidence. But I was very astonished to learn that the commissioner also knew the secret of a special, and very difficult, mission.

During this interval the armament was pursued without interruption. The commissioner purchased at Nantes a former merchantman called *la Pallas* of 32 eight-pounders and a small

---

[32] The object of Jones' distaste was Jacques Donatien Le Ray, sieur de Chaumont. Jones, who refers to Chaumont as "the commissioner," believed that Chaumont was attempting to obstruct his mission and ruin his reputation. Chaumont to Jones, February 17, 1779; Jones to Benjamin Franklin, October 3, 1779, and July 12, 1780; all in the Jones Papers. See also Morison, *Jones*, pp. 197–99, 338–41. The "Concordat" that Jones claimed Chaumont forced him to sign is printed in Wharton, *Diplomatic Correspondence*, 4:305–6.

[33] Ultimately Lafayette returned to America without participating in Jones' planned raid on England, but his real interest in the project can be seen in Benjamin Franklin to Lafayette, March 22, 1779, and Franklin to the Committee of Foreign Affairs, May 26, 1779. Wharton, *Diplomatic Correspondence*, 3:91–92, 187–88.

brig called *la Vengeance* of 12 three-pounders. Neither of these two ships had been built for war. They proceeded to Lorient to join the *Bonhomme Richard*, as did *le Cerf*, a very handsome cutter from the royal navy of 18 nine-pound cannon, and the *Alliance*, a completely new frigate, belonging to the United States, mounting 36 guns. Because the cannon had not yet arrived from Angoulême, the *Bonhomme Richard* was armed with an old battery of 12-pounders, and as the aim of the project was the enemy's main ports, I mounted six old 18-pound cannon over *the powder magazine*, so that the *Bonhomme Richard*, which strictly speaking was a frigate of 34 guns, now carried 40. As it was impossible to procure a sufficient number of American sailors, it was decided to remedy this deficiency by enrolling sailors who were prisoners of war in France, and *marine companies* were hurriedly formed by drafting a certain number of peasants. So it is easy to understand that the *Bonhomme Richard* had one of the worst crews ever found on a vessel. But I had been told that a body of elite troops under the marquis de Lafayette would guarantee the good conduct of the crew. However, when the small squadron was ready for service and the troops were ready to embark, I received a letter from the marquis de Lafayette in which he informed me that the purpose of the expedition having been divulged in Paris, the king had ordered that the troops not embark. The marquis de Lafayette was ordered to join his regiment.

Thus the project, which was no less than raiding Liverpool, the second largest city of England, failed because it had been indiscreetly communicated to ____.

It has been noted that the first plan to arm my little squadron called for two fireships and 500 men from the Régiment de Walsh Irlandais as landing troops. But the minister did not keep his word; he neither procured the fireships nor the 500 troops, so it was impossible for me to carry out the plan I had developed with M. Garnier, which in my opinion was even more important than raiding Liverpool. The commissioner was not only indiscreet but at Lorient he assumed the role of minister, and by interfering consistently in the discipline of the squadron he led the captains and officers to turn to him on all occasions as *a subject of France representing the king's person* and to consider me with a suspicious eye as a *foreigner*.

In my opinion, it was hardly possible for the commissioner

to render a greater disservice to his country, because the king had generously resolved to sustain, at his expense and under the American flag, the squadron he had entrusted to me; and as I had given all the commissions to the American officers, it was important for the good of the service that they believe they were in the pay and service of Congress and that the squadron belonged to the United States. If the officers had been of this belief, one could have expected very outstanding services despite the disadvantages of poor crews, bad cannon, and vessels that were not designed for war. But because doubt and jealousy were cast into their minds, all subordination was destroyed.

I received orders to escort from Lorient a fleet of transports and merchantmen bound for different ports between that city and Bordeaux, and after that I was to take, or to chase the English from, the Bay of Biscay and then return to Lorient for further orders.

While fulfilling this mission, as the squadron and the convoy were laying to at night with topsails aback at the latitude of Rochefort, the *Bonhomme Richard* and the *Alliance* ran afoul of each other and suffered minor damage. As this accident occurred through the negligence of the officers on watch, they were cashiered and discharged from the service.[34]

I gave chase to several vessels, but I was unable to overtake them. One morning I saw three frigates, a light squadron from Rochefort under the command of the chevalier de la Touche, which were to the windward. Since *le Cerf* had given chase to a ship the preceding day until it was lost from view, I had only the *Bonhomme Richard*, the *Alliance*, and *la Pallas* with *la Vengeance*, a small corvette of so little consequence she was hardly worth counting. I believed that the squadron I had in view was English and I made every effort to reach it, but without success.

A few days later, finding myself in view of the Isle de Groix, I permitted the vessels that were under my orders to go to Lorient as quickly as possible. The weather was foggy and in the afternoon I found myself alone on the *Bonhomme Richard* and very near two frigates which began pursuing me. As soon

---

[34] Robert Robinson, the first lieutenant of the *Bonhomme Richard*, was court-martialed and adjudged "guilty of negligence of duty." Lorenz, *Jones*, pp. 261–62.

as I was ready to do battle, and seeing that they were faster than the *Bonhomme Richard*, I put about to go into combat. But when they saw this they also put about. I crowded sail on and followed them until after midnight; they were then beyond Belle-Isle, and because of their superior speed they were nearly out of sight.

The chevalier de la Touche, who commanded them from the frigate *l'Hermione*, dropped anchor three or four days later at Isle de Groix and sent his boat to Lorient to pay his compliments. He had taken me for English both times he had encountered me.

While the *Bonhomme Richard* and the *Alliance* were being repaired at Lorient, I sent *la Pallas*, *le Cerf*, and *la Vengeance* to patrol in the Bay of Biscay to protect the coast and to take or chase any enemy ships that were cruising there.

The commissioner had again come to Lorient from the court under the pretext of better equipping the *Bonhomme Richard*, but his real aim was to form a new conspiracy that would force me to sign an agreement with the captains to send all of the squadron's prizes into port *under his consignment*. This grasping man had the skill to persuade the captains that if they did this they would restrain me and that their interests would be more secure in his hands.

The commissioner persuaded Mr. Franklin that the king's intention was that the prizes be sent into port to be at his (the commissioner's) disposition and the American minister gave me orders to that effect.

By this order, contrary to the laws governing the use of the American flag, Mr. Franklin exceeded the limits of authority that Congress had confided in him.

When the squadron was ready to put to sea and the captains had signed the Concordat, the commissioner pretended to have received extraordinary authority from the minister of marine, whereby he could, if he determined that it was appropriate, remove the commander of the squadron. As a result I felt it was prudent to sign the Concordat and I signed it on the eve of my departure. At any other time and in any other circumstances, I would have rejected this condition with disdain. I saw the danger I ran, but having announced in America that I was remaining in Europe, because the French court had requested this, to command some secret expedition,

I resolved to expose myself to all dangers.

Although other American prisoners had arrived at Nantes after having been exchanged in England, I could only make a very small change in the crew of the *Bonhomme Richard*. They were generally so mean that the only expedient I could find that allowed me to command was to divide them into two parties and let one group of rogues guard the other.

I received orders to sail west of Ireland and north of Scotland to intercept the enemy shipping around the Orcades, the Cape of Derneus, and Dogger Bank and to return to the Texel by October 1 to receive further orders. But as I had informed Dr. Franklin, through whom I had always received the orders of the court, this so limited my operations that I would not be able to take advantage of circumstances which might permit me to render more important services, such as intercepting commerce of much greater importance, making a landing and alarming the enemy in the north, and making a considerable diversion on behalf of the comte d'Orvilliers, who was in the channel with 66 ships of the line with which he was expected to destroy Plymouth or Portsmouth and perhaps both of them.[35] Mr. Franklin, as a result, gave me carte blanche for six weeks for these operations, and the only restriction he maintained was that I was to enter the Texel by the first of October.

In addition to various ideas I had, I was informed from England that eight vessels were expected from India and that they should first appear off the west coast of Ireland near Limerick. This merited attention. As there were two privateers at Lorient ready for sea, *le Monsieur* of 40 guns and *le Granville* of 14, whose officers had already offered to place themselves under my command, I agreed to their proposition. But the commissioner would not hear of accepting any engagement from them regarding their conduct.

This arrogant action caused the spread of the belief among the Americans, and particularly on board the *Alliance*, that the squadron belonged neither to the king of France nor to Congress

---

[35] The Franco-Spanish "invasion" of England and its diplomatic effects are discussed in Jonathan R. Dull, *The French Navy and American Independence: A Study of Arms and Diplomacy, 1774–1787* (Princeton: Princeton University Press, 1975), pp. 143–58; and in Richard Morris, *The Peacemakers; the Great Powers and American Independence* (New York: Harper & Row, 1965), pp. 27–42.

but to the owners of privateers with whom the commissioner and Dr. Franklin were associated.

With all these mishaps, it is easy to see that I was thwarted in all my projects and that my situation was perhaps the most precarious and the most disagreeable in which a commander had ever found himself.

The squadron set sail from the Groix roadstead on August 14, 1779. As soon as I had passed to the north of the entrance of the channel, the two corsairs *le Monsieur* and *le Granville* abandoned me during the night, and *le Cerf* was separated immediately after. I had wanted to wait for the ships from India for 15 days at the latitude of Limerick; but the captain of the *Alliance*, who pretended to believe the rest of the squadron were privateers, made a great deal of difficulty and then left me during the night.[36]

Because I then had only *la Pallas* and *la Vengeance* with me, I was obliged to renounce my plans concerning the eight ships from India. From the beginning I had not counted on the two privateers; but I naturally expected the *Alliance* and *le Cerf* to rendezvous north of Scotland. The *Alliance* rejoined me, but *le Cerf* returned to France.

I had taken two prizes near Ireland, which I sent to France. Within sight of Scotland I captured two *privateers*, valuable ships of 32 guns each, and a brigantine, which I sent to Bergen in Norway in accordance with the order I had received from Dr. Franklin. These three prizes were restored to England by the king of Denmark. The *Alliance* left me again when I entered the North Sea. I captured several prizes near the Gulf of Edinburgh, and I learned from speaking to the prisoners and from the newspapers that were on board the prizes that the capital of Scotland and the port of Leith were undefended. The newspapers also confirmed the word I had received from England concerning the eight ships from India; they had entered the port of Limerick three days after I had been obliged to leave the harbor's entrance.

---

[36] Pierre Landais commanded the *Alliance*. Apparently Landais was trying to make Jones look bad. See Morison, *Jones*, pp. 208–9, 293–301; Landais to Jones, June 16, 1779, and Jones to Franklin, October 3, 1779, both in the Jones Papers; and John Adams, *Diary and Autobiography of John Adams*, ed. Lyman H. Butterfield et al., 4 vols. (Cambridge: Belknap Press of Harvard University Press, 1961), 2:363–79, ad passim. For a daily record of the *Bonhomme Richard*'s activities during this voyage, see *The Log of the Bon Homme Richard* (Mystic, Conn.: Marine Historical Association, Inc., 1936), pp. 23–47.

Because of the situation at Edinburgh and at Leith (which had only a coastguard vessel of 20 guns and two cutters to defend the roads), I believed it would be possible to put Leith and Edinburgh under ransom.[37] I had only the *Bonhomme Richard, la Pallas,* and *la Vengeance* with which to execute this great project. But I knew that to strike a brilliant blow it was not always necessary to have a great force. I convinced the captains of *la Pallas* and the small corvette,[38] by holding out the prospect of large profits to them. I was sure that in case of failure I could still, at least, make a very advantageous diversion in behalf of the enterprise of the comte d'Orvilliers in the *channel.* I distributed red uniforms to my marines, and I placed a few men dressed in them on the two prizes so that the two ships looked like transports.

The necessary arrangements were taken to carry out the enterprise, but a quarter of an hour before the attack was to have been made a sudden storm rose and obliged me to run before the wind out of the Gulf of Edinburgh. The storm was so violent it sent one of my prizes to the bottom.[39]

I had in mind other enterprises which, despite the mediocrity of my force, could be executed on the west coast of Great Britain. But I could not persuade the captains of *la Pallas* and *la Vengeance* to support me. I was therefore obliged to limit myself to spreading alarm and destroying shipping, and I fulfilled this dual aim all along the coast to Hull. In this manner I made a very considerable diversion, and I drew English forces toward me, thus greatly favoring the enterprise of the combined fleet at Plymouth and Portsmouth.

On the morning of September 23, while I was cruising at the latitude of the Cape of Flamborough, which I had assigned

---

[37] Jones had planned to demand a £100,000 indemnity. Jones, "Instructions to Captain Paul de Chamillard," September 14, 1779; Jones to the provost of Leith, September 14, 1779; both in the Jones Papers. Jones' raids struck fear into many coastal communities of Great Britain. For example, Hull's great trepidations and hurried preparations are evident in a letter of the marquis of Rockingham, vice admiral of Yorkshire. Rockingham to Lord Weymouth, September 28, 1779, printed in *American Historical Review* 15 (April 1910): 567–71.

[38] Denis Nicolas Cottineau de Kerloguen commanded *La Pallas* and Philippe Nicolas Ricot commanded *la Vengeance.* Jones, "List of Officers of Auxiliary Vessels Under Command Of," May 1–3, 1779, Jones Papers.

[39] Jones sailed within cannon shot of Leith and was ready to launch his boats when a strong gale sprang up and drove him to the mouth of the Firth of Forth. Morison, *Jones,* pp. 212–20.

for my third rendezvous, and where I expected to be rejoined by the *Alliance* and *le Cerf* and to meet the Baltic fleet which was expected at any hour, the *Alliance* appeared but she did not speak to the *Bonhomme Richard.*

I had put men on several *prizes*, and I had lost two boats with their crews who had fled to the coast of Ireland. At that moment I had sent the second lieutenant ⟦Henry Lunt⟧ with another officer and 18 men in a pilot boat to chase a ship then in view to the windward. As a result my crew was very diminished and on the *Bonhomme Richard* I had only one lieutenant ⟦Richard Dale⟧ and some junior officers.

I was in these circumstances when the Baltic fleet appeared toward 2 P.M. I was windward of the enemy and two leagues from the coast of England.

Information from prisoners had confirmed that the fleet was escorted by the *Serapis*, a new vessel that could mount 56 guns but then mounted only 44 in two batteries, one composed of 18-pounders, and by the *Countess of Scarborough*, a new frigate mounting 22 guns.

When the enemy saw that we had taken the chase, the *Serapis* and the *Countess of Scarborough* took advantage of the wind to stand out to sea while the convoy crowded on sail toward the fortress of Scarborough.

As there was little wind, I was unable to close with the enemy before night. The moon did not rise until 8 o'clock, and as soon as it was dark the *Serapis* and the *Countess of Scarborough* came about and put on all sail for the fort of Scarborough.

I was fortunate enough to discover this enemy movement with my night glass, otherwise they would have escaped me. As this forced me to alter my course by six points of the compass with the intention of cutting off the enemy from their retreat toward shore, the captain of *la Pallas* concluded that the crew of the *Bonhomme Richard* had revolted, and this idea convinced him to haul his wind and to stand away from the shore.[40] At the same time, the *Alliance* lay windward of the enemy at a considerable distance. Because the captain of this vessel had not paid attention to the signals of the *Bonhomme*

---

[40] See Jones to Franklin, October 3, 1779, and Jones, "Account of Engagement with *Serapis*," September 25, 1779, in the Jones Papers.

Richard since leaving France, I was obliged to run all the risks and engage the enemy with the *Bonhomme Richard* alone to prevent their escape.

I began the battle at 7 o'clock at night and within pistol range of the *Serapis*, and I sustained it for nearly an hour at that distance, exposed at the same time to the attack of the *Countess of Scarborough*, which raked the stern of the *Bonhomme Richard* with broadsides.

It has been noted that properly speaking the *Bonhomme Richard* was only a frigate of 34 guns, the battery of which was of 12-pounders; but that it had been decided to mount six 18-pounders above the *powder magazine*, which would have been very useful in cannonading a port. The sea was very calm during the battle with the *Serapis* and I hoped to derive a great advantage from these six 18-pound guns. But instead of that, the old cannons burst at the beginning of the action and the officers and men above the powder magazine, who had been selected as the best of the crew, were killed, wounded, or so frightened that none of them was of any use during the remainder of the engagement.

In this unfortunate extremity, having to contend with forces three times superior to my own, the *Bonhomme Richard* was in great danger of going to the bottom. With her battery out of action I had recourse to the dangerous expedient of throwing grappling irons on the *Serapis* in order to nullify the superior power of her two batteries and to shield myself from the fire of the *Countess of Scarborough*. This maneuver succeeded perfectly, and with my own hands I tied the *Serapis* to the *Bonhomme Richard*. The captain [Thomas Piercy] of the *Countess of Scarborough*, an illegitimate son of the duke of Northumberland, conducted himself like a man of sense and from that time on ceased fire on the *Bonhomme Richard*, knowing full well that he could not damage us without equally damaging the *Serapis*.

The *Serapis* being then to windward, dropped her anchor as soon as she was hooked, hoping by this to disengage herself from the *Bonhomme Richard*, but success did not answer her expectations. From then on the combat was limited to the firing of cannon, swivel guns, muskets, and grenades. The enemy at first showed a desire to board the *Bonhomme Richard;* however, after having thought it over, they did not dare try. But the

33

Serapis had the advantage of her two batteries, besides the cannon on the quarterdeck and on the forecastle, whereas the *Bonhomme Richard's* cannon were either broken or abandoned, except for four pieces on the quarterdeck, which were also abandoned for some minutes. The officer [Matthew Mease] who commanded these four cannons on the quarterdeck was danger-ously wounded in the head, and having at that moment no object more deserving of my attention, I took command of them myself. Some sailors came to aid me of their own accord and serviced the two cannon alongside of the enemy with surprising skill and courage. A few minutes later I found enough men to transport one of the cannon on the quarterdeck to the opposite side, but I was not able to find sufficient force to bring the other, so I could bring to bear only three guns against the enemy for the rest of the action.

The moon rose at 8 o'clock in the evening and the two vessels were then in flames from the cannonade. That was why the *Serapis'* mainmast, which was painted yellow, was such an easy object to distinguish, and I pointed one of my guns loaded with bar shot at it. In the meantime the two other pieces were well used to destroy the barricades of the enemy and to sweep their quarterdeck with oblique fire. Only the men on the topmast bravely supported the quarterdeck cannons with muskets and swivel guns and threw grenades on board the enemy vessel with great skill.

In this way the enemy were killed, wounded, or driven from their stations on deck and aloft, notwithstanding the superiority of their artillery and manpower.

The captain [Richard Pearson] of the *Serapis* consulted with his officers and they resolved to surrender, but an un-fortunate circumstance happened on board the *Bonhomme Richard* to prevent them. A bullet having cut one of our pumps, the master carpenter [John Gunnison] was seized with panic and cried to the chief gunner [Henry Gardner] and the master at arms [John Burbank] "that the *Bonhomme Richard* was sinking." This idea so terrified these men that they forgot their duties and thought only of saving their lives. At the same moment, someone told the chief gunner that the lieutenant and I had been killed. As a result, thinking that he had become the commanding officer, the chief gunner rushed to the bridge to haul down the American flag, which he would have done if the

34

flagstaff had not been carried away when the *Bonhomme Richard* hooked the *Serapis*.

The captain of the *Serapis*, hearing the chief gunner of the *Bonhomme Richard* ask for quarter because he thought the *Bonhomme Richard* was sinking, hastened to cry to me: "*Do you ask for quarter? Do you ask for quarter?*"

I had been so occupied in firing the three cannon on the quarterdeck, I did not know what had passed between the chief gunner, the master carpenter, and the master at arms, so that I replied to the English captain: "*Je ne songe point à me rendre, mais je suis déterminé à vous faire demander quartier.*"[41]

The captain of the *Serapis*, however, conceived some hope, because of what the American chief gunner had said, *that the Bonhomme Richard was about to sink*. But when he found that his men on the upper decks were in imminent danger, he sent them to the main deck to service the two batteries, which they fired against the side of the *Bonhomme Richard* with the fury of vengeance and despair.

It has been observed that, when I began the action, *la Pallas* was a great distance to the windward and the *Alliance* also lay to the windward. When the captain of *la Pallas* heard action begin, he approached and spoke to the *Alliance*, but they lost much time and it was not until after all that has been related that the two frigates came within cannon range of the *Countess of Scarborough*. Because *la Pallas* engaged this frigate while sailing before the wind and tide (at the same time that the *Serapis* was at anchor and under the grappling irons of the *Bonhomme Richard*, which had the wind astern), soon they were both a considerable distance to leeward. The *Alliance* followed *la Pallas* and the *Countess of Scarborough* and while passing along the exterior side of the *Bonhomme Richard* delivered a broadside within gunshot range against the bow of this frigate and the stern of the *Serapis*, which together formed one small target. But it is easy to suppose that the broadside of the *Alliance* did more damage to the *Bonhomme Richard* than to the *Serapis* because the men of the *Serapis* had been chased

---

[41] Morison, *Jones*, p. 236, translates this as "No, sir, I haven't as yet thought of it, but I'm determined to make you strike." H. Niles in *Niles' Weekly Register* 2 (July 4, 1812): 297, translates it as "I do not dream of surrendering, but I am determined to make you strike." The more popular version—"I have not yet begun to fight"—was recorded by Richard Dale for a biography in 1825.

je répondis au Capitaine Anglais:" Je ne songe
"point à me rendre, mais je suis déterminé à
"vous faire demander quartier."

Le Capitaine du Serapis cependant, conçut
l'espérance, par les paroles qu'il avoit entendu dire
au maître Canonier américain, que le Bon-homme
Richard étoit près à couler à fond; mais comme il
trouva que ses hommes servient en trop grand danger
sur les gaillards, il les envoya sous le pont, pour
servir aux deux batteries, qu'ils déchargèrent ensuite
contre le côté du Bon-homme Richard avec tant de
fureur qu'elle indiquoit tout à la fois la vengeance
et le désespoir.

Il a été observé que la Pallas quand je
commençai l'action étoit à une grande distance
au vent, et que l'Alliance étoit aussi en panne au
vent. Lorsque le Capitaine de la Pallas entendit
l'action s'engager, il s'approcha et parla à l'Alliance,
mais ils perdirent au longtems, et ce ne fut qu'après
tous ce qui vinrent d'être rapporté que ces deux frégates
vinrent à la portée du canon de la Comtesse de
Scarborough. Comme la Pallas engagea cette
frégate vent arrière et avant la marée (pendant
que le Serapis étoit à l'ancre et sous les Grapins

from the upper decks to the covered deck; whereas on board the *Bonhomme Richard* not only a number of people who were then on the upper decks (after they had been chased by the two enemy batteries from the places where they were hidden) but also the men who were serving the pumps and the three guns on the quarterdeck were much more exposed.

The battle between the *Bonhomme Richard* and the *Serapis* continued with the greatest intensity. The bulwarks of the *Serapis* were damaged or burned, and the mainmast was gradually cut down by the grapeshot of the *Bonhomme Richard*, while the much superior artillery of the *Serapis*' two batteries struck one side of the *Bonhomme Richard* and blew out the other so that during the last hour of combat the shot passed through both sides of the *Bonhomme Richard* meeting little or no resistance. The rudder was shattered and only an old timber here and there kept the poop from crashing down on the *gundeck*.

After a retreating action of short duration the *Countess of Scarborough* surrendered to *la Pallas*. They were then a considerable distance to the leeward of the *Bonhomme Richard* and the *Serapis*. The *Alliance*, which had followed them downwind, lost much time in going this way and that and questioning *the prize* and *la Pallas*, but finally the captain of *la Pallas* asked the captain of the *Alliance*: "*Do you want to take charge of the prize, or go to aid the commodore?*" and the *Alliance* began to maneuver to gain the wind. She tacked several times before regaining the wind and finally she sent a second broadside against the bow of the *Serapis* and the stern of the *Bonhomme Richard*. Some other people and I shouted to the *Alliance* to cease firing for God's sake and to send some men on board the *Bonhomme Richard*. The captain of the *Alliance* disobeyed; passing alongside the *Bonhomme Richard* and bringing a few cannon to bear during the passage, she unleashed a third broadside against the bow of the *Bonhomme Richard* and the stern of the *Serapis*. After this the *Alliance* kept at a respectful distance and took great care not to expose herself either to receive a blow or to have a single man killed or wounded.[42]

The idea that the *Bonhomme Richard* was going to sink

---

[42] Affidavits of midshipmen Nathaniel Fanning, John Mayrant, Robert Coram, and J. W. Linthwaite, dated October 23, 24, and 27, 1779, substantiating Jones' account of the *Alliance's* perfidy, are in PCC, item 162, 2:153–64.

had so deranged the master at arms' mind by excessive fear that he opened the hatches and, despite my repeated orders to the contrary, let out all of the prisoners we had, numbering 100. At the time of outfitting, the commissioner had refused to provide iron chains for the prisoners, and this mental derange-ment of the master at arms might have become fatal, if I had not taken advantage of the prisoners' fear and put them to work at the pumps where they displayed surprising zeal, appearing to have forgotten that they were prisoners and that nothing could prevent their leaving the *Bonhomme Richard* to board the *Serapis*, as it was entirely in their power to put an end to the fight by killing me or throwing me overboard.

As the three guns of the *Bonhomme Richard* continued to fire without interruption against the *Serapis* and finally cut down the railing on her quarterdeck and her mainmast, so that the latter was only supported by the yards of the *Bonhomme Richard*, and at the same time the men in the rigging maintained a continuous fire of muskets, swivel guns, and grenades, the enemy began to slacken their fire and soon lost all hope. One circumstance that contributed a great deal to the victory of the *Bonhomme Richard* was the extraordinary presence of mind and intrepidity of a Scottish sailor [William Hamilton] who was posted in the *mainmast*. This brave man, on his own accord, seized a lighted match and a basket of grenades and advanced along the main yard of the *Bonhomme Richard* until he was directly over the enemy's upper deck, and as the flames from their railings and shrouds added to the light of the moon he could see all that happened on the enemy vessel. Every time he saw two or three men gathered together he would throw a grenade among them. He was even skillful enough to throw several into their hatchways, and one of them set fire to the charge of an 18-pounder on the first gundeck, burning a number of people.

At this point the captain of the *Serapis* advanced on the upper deck, lowered his flag, and asked for quarter. At the very instant that he was lowering his flag, his mainmast fell into the sea. He came with his officers from the *Serapis* onto the *Bon-homme Richard* and presented me with his sword. While this was happening 8 or 10 men of the *Bonhomme Richard* made off with the *Serapis'* shallop, which had been in tow during the fight.

It was after 11 o'clock when the battle ended; consequently, it had lasted more than four hours. The *Bonhomme Richard* had on board only 322 men, good or bad, when the battle began; and the 60 men who were stationed in the powder magazine when the cannon burst, having been of no service during the action, cannot properly be counted as part of the force that opposed the *Serapis*. While in Denmark the *Serapis* had received a number of English sailors who had come from India to that country, so that according to the roll, which was found after the battle, there were more than 400 men on board when she first encountered the *Bonhomme Richard*.

Her superiority in cannon was even greater, not to mention the intrinsic value of her artillery, which so completely surpassed that of the *Bonhomme Richard* that it would be very difficult to compare them.

Thus, putting aside the damage done to the *Bonhomme Richard* by the *Countess of Scarborough* during the first hour of combat and by the three broadsides of the *Alliance* thereafter, it is not difficult to form a judgment on the combat between the *Bonhomme Richard* and the *Serapis* and on a victory obtained over so superior a force after such a long, bloody, and close-range battle.[43]

La Vengeance, a corvette mounting 12 three-pounders, and the pilot's boat with the second lieutenant [Henry Lunt] of the *Bonhomme Richard*, another officer, and 18 men, could have been of singular service either in pursuing and capturing the convoy, or in reinforcing me by supplementing the men on board the *Bonhomme Richard*. But, strange to say! they remained all the time as spectators without interest in the affair, staying out of danger and to windward, and the least that one can say about the conduct of the *Alliance* is that it appeared to stem from a principle worse than ignorance or insubordination.

---

[43] Jones' description of the battle is by all accounts accurate except for some minor discrepancies. For example, the *Serapis* was carrying 50 guns, not 44; the *Bonhomme Richard* had 40 guns; and the *Countess of Scarborough*, 20 guns. Morison, *Jones*, p. 226. For another description by Jones of this voyage and battle, see Jones to Franklin, October 3, 1779 (18 pp.), Jones Papers. Pearson's account of the battle differs only slightly from that of Jones. Pearson insisted that the *Alliance* severely damaged his ship and was a major cause for his defeat. Pearson's and Piercy's accounts of the fight and records of the subsequent court-martial that praised them for their stiff defense against a superior force are in the Public Record Office, Admiralty I, Captains' Dispatches, vol. 2305, and Reports of Courts-martial, vol. 5315.

It is clear from what has been said that if the Baltic fleet escaped, it is due particularly to the disorder that the commissioner created in the squadron through his avaricious cabals. And one can attribute the impossibility of waiting for the eight vessels from India and the fact that no enemy ports were destroyed or ransomed to this same cause.

It is fair to say, however, that some of the officers who were on board the *Bonhomme Richard* conducted themselves in a very admirable manner during the action. The lieutenant (Richard Dale) having been abandoned at the battery and finding that he could not rally his men, came up on deck, and, although wounded, supervised the working of the pumps. But despite all his efforts, the hold of the *Bonhomme Richard* was more than half filled with water when the enemy surrendered.

During the last three hours of the battle, the two vessels were on fire. Quantities of water were thrown on it and the fire at times appeared to be extinguished, but it always broke out anew. After the action, it was thought to be entirely extinguished. The weather was calm during the remainder of the night, but when the wind rose a little the fire broke out again, much more dangerous for having penetrated the timbers of the *Bonhomme Richard* to within a few inches of the powder magazines. The powder was immediately carried on deck, ready to be thrown into the sea as a last resort. Finally the fire was completely extinguished by our cutting away planks and drowning it with great amounts of water.

The next morning the weather was cloudy and foggy, and when it cleared around 11 o'clock all of the enemy convoy had taken refuge under the fortress of Scarborough and not a single sail was to be seen along the coast.

We then examined the *Bonhomme Richard* to determine if it were possible for her to be conducted into some port. The examination ended at 6 o'clock in the evening, and we judged the thing impracticable, mostly because of blows she had received in the bow from the *Alliance*, causing holes that could not be closed. Consequently, I employed all the boats without delay to save the wounded by carrying them to other vessels. This work took all night, and the next morning, despite our having continuously and vigorously employed the pumps, the water had entirely filled the hold. Then, as the wind rose, the *Bonhomme Richard* immediately sank.

I saved only my signal flags. I lost all of my belongings, amounting to more than 50,000 livres, not counting a number of invaluable papers. The officers and men of the ship also lost all of their personal effects.

I took command of the *Serapis*, on which we had rigged jury masts, but I was tossed about in the North Sea by contrary winds for 10 days before reaching the Texel. I would have liked first to debark my 600 prisoners at Dunkirk, and the wind was favorable for this enterprise the day I entered the Texel. But the commissioner's cabal opposed this necessary plan. Because that imprudent man had told the captains not only that the squadron was destined for the Texel, but also what its object was to be in Holland, they left me, and I was obliged to follow them into the Texel since they had most of the prisoners.

Upon my entry into the Texel, I found the agent of Congress (M. Dumas) from whom I received the orders of the minister of marine in a letter from Dr. Franklin. I found by these letters that I had received a very important assignment: it was nothing less than to escort from there to Brest some 100 Dutch vessels loaded with war materiel and building timbers belonging to His Majesty.[44]

It also seemed to be the intention of the minister that I take the officers and men of the *Bonhomme Richard* to man the new frigate *l'Indienne*, which carried a battery of 36-pounders and which, as I have already observed, had been built in Amsterdam for the United States.

Although this matter concerning *l'Indienne* was the only one that had been communicated to me before leaving France, the entire project had been revealed to the commissioner, and I think that, as was his wont, to ease the burden of this confidence he had passed it on to all the captains, and possibly even to a great number of his personal friends. Because the captains talked about it in Holland without any reserve, immediately after my arrival I thought it was my duty to inform the minister that I foresaw the impossibility of executing this plan. It is obvious that if the commissioner had not intervened with his

---

[44] This convoy waited for Jones to escort it to France, but it had to remain at the Texel until the navy of the United Provinces could provide an escort. The British navy attacked it and provided an immediate occasion for a mutual declaration of war between Great Britain and Holland. Morison, *Jones*, p. 265.

cabal in this project, I would have entered the Texel with my entire squadron little damaged.

The events that followed proved my conjecture was right. The grand allied fleet of 66 vessels of the line having retired from the channel without attempting a single military operation, Great Britain was reassured as to her fear of invasion and turned a great part of her attention to the vengeance she desired to exercise on me. For this purpose she employed 42 sail, some two-decked vessels but most simply frigates. This force was divided into light squadrons, one of which was stationed in the Downs to keep watch on the strait between Dover and Calais. The English cruised the length of the eastern coast of England and Scotland, advanced to the coast of Norway, patrolled the sea of Ireland and the west coast of that island, and, as soon as my presence in Holland was known in England, two squadrons were sent to watch the entrance of the Texel and the Fly. They never left these posts during the remainder of the three months that I was in Holland.[45]

My situation in the Texel greatly influenced the policies of all the belligerent powers and captivated the attention of all of Europe.

England's ambassador to The Hague [Sir Joseph Yorke] addressed different memorials to the Estates General, insisting on the return of the *Serapis* and the *Countess of Scarborough* to his king and claiming me as "*the Scottish pirate*," but these memorials did not have the effect he desired, and the efforts he made to induce some magistrates or citizens of Amsterdam to betray or kidnap me were equally without success.[46]

It was necessary to repair the squadron and to procure a mainmast for the *Serapis* and provisions from Amsterdam for about 600 prisoners. Because it was very difficult to treat the wounded on board the ships, the Estates General allowed me to

---

[45] *The London Chronicle* reported on October 14 that two squadrons which had pursued Jones had returned to the Downs. *The London Chronicle*, October 12–14, 1779. But other reports listed 16 ships in pursuit of Jones. For other newspapers accounts related to the exploits of Jones and the *Bonhomme Richard* see *The London Chronicle*, September 21–23, 25–28, 28–30, and October 12–14, 1779; and Seitz, *Paul Jones*, pp. 29–147. For a highly exaggerated contemporary biography of Jones, see Theophilus Smart, *Authentic Memoirs of Captain Paul Jones, the American Corsair* . . . (London: A. Hogg, 1779).

[46] Joseph Yorke to the States-General, October 29, 1779, in Wharton, *Diplomatic Correspondence*, 3:396–97. Additional details of Ambassador Yorke's efforts to secure Jones' arrest or expulsion are in Daniel A. Miller, *Sir Joseph Yorke and Anglo-Dutch Relations, 1774–1780* (The Hague: Mouton & Co., Printers, 1970), pp. 78–87.

use the fort on the Island of Texel for this purpose. These circumstances, and particularly that of the fort in the Texel, infuriated the English government and put Holland in a situation so critical that the Estates General were obliged to insist that I should either leave the Texel or produce a commis' sion from His Most Christian Majesty and remain thereafter under the French flag.

On this occasion, the prince of Orange sent Vice Admiral Rhynst to take command of the Dutch fleet in the Texel, which was composed of 13 double-decked warships. The prince knew this would give great pleasure to the English court, because M. Rhynst was an Englishman at heart.

While these arrangements were being made, I reembarked the wounded, who had been cared for in the fort, and I made all preparations to make sail for Dunkirk with my prizes and prisoners. But the duc de la Vauguyon[47] granted me an interview at Amsterdam and informed me that the intention of the king was that the vessels should remain in the Texel under the French flag because their capture by the enemy was thought to be certain if they should hazard putting to sea. His Excellency said everything he could to convince me to accept a commission which had been sent for that purpose from Versailles. Not having the legal authority to change my flag and dishonor myself by disavowing my first declaration, I refused this honor, because I had made a declaration as an *American officer* and had given a copy of my commission from Congress to the Dutch officer who commanded in the Texel. To have accepted the flag of France when I found myself between a crossfire in the Texel would have been to lose for His Most Christian Majesty all the merit of having placed the squadron under the flag of his allies. We dare say that it had never been unfurled with more glory than on this occasion. But although I had no other instructions from Dr. Franklin than to deliver all of my prisoners to the duc de la Vauguyon, still this obliged me to put the *Serapis* and

---

[47] When Jones met the French minister at The Hague, Paul François de Quelen, duc de la Vauguyon, he agreed to tell the Dutch commandant that he had a French commission. See Vauguyon to Jones, October 29, 1779, and Jones to Vauguyon, October 5 and November 4, 1779, Jones Papers; Wharton, *Diplomatic Correspondence*, 3:396–98.

The actions of Jones' ships in the Texel and during his subsequent return to France are chronicled in the logbooks of the *Serapis* and *Alliance*. John S. Barnes, ed., *The Logs of the Serapis—Alliance—Ariel Under the Command of John Paul Jones, 1779–1780* (New York: Printed for the Naval History Society by De Vinne Press, 1911), pp. 25–90.

the *Countess of Scarborough* under his orders because *la Pallas* and *la Vengeance* could not hold all the prisoners.[48]

It should be noted that on this occasion, before the eyes of all Europe, I made a sacrifice much greater than that made by any other officer in the Revolution. I sacrificed the military pride that forbids an officer to leave his prizes or his prisoners, taken at such great cost, in a neutral port. It is recognized that under American maritime laws prizes belong exclusively to those who take them.

The captain of the *Alliance*, a congressional frigate, having received orders from Dr. Franklin to return to Paris to answer for his conduct according to the wishes of the king, and finding myself with authority to do so, I sent on board the *Alliance* the rest of the officers and American crewmen of the *Bonhomme Richard* who had been transferred to the *Serapis*. Then, taking command of the *Alliance*, I continued to display the American flag while the rest of the squadron and the prizes flew that of France.[49]

M. Rhynst did what the prince of Orange expected of him: he placed and kept his squadron in the best tactical position during the 6-week period after I came on board when storms and contrary winds forced the *Alliance* to remain in the Texel. M. Rhynst, in a word, did all that he could, and more than would have been expected of an honest man, to make my situation dangerous and disagreeable.

Finally the wind became favorable, and on December 27, 1779, the *Alliance* made sail at 10 o'clock in the morning, having lost all her anchors but one because of the ill will of M. Rhynst, who had ordered the Dutch pilot to allow the *Alliance* only one anchor. Thus, departing from the Texel I did not leave a friend in M. Rhynst, and as I put to sea the odds were a hundred to one that we would soon have a serious affair with the enemy. I was, however, fortunate enough to escape from their vigilance,

---

[48] The *Countess of Scarborough, la Vengeance,* and two other French cutters returned 191 English prisoners to England but exchanged them for French rather than American prisoners, to Jones' anger and indignation. See Franklin to Jones, October 15, 1779, and March 25, 1784, Jones Papers; Morison, *Jones,* p. 263.

[49] On these points see Admiral Reynst to Jones, December 17, 1779, and Jones to Reynst, December 17, 1779; Jones to the duc de la Vauguyon, December 13, 1779; Jones to Franklin, December 13, 1779; and Dumas to the Committee of Foreign Affairs, Wharton, *Diplomatic Correspondence,* 3:423–26, 430.

by hugging the coast and passing to the windward between them and the coast of Flanders. The next day I passed the straits of Calais to the windward, within sight of the vessels that cruised there and the squadron stationed near the Downs. The following day I saw the fleet at Portsmouth, and I passed near several cruisers. On January 1, I left the channel.

At the latitude of Hull, I had taken a pilot [John Jackson] who subsequently conducted himself very well. This poor man had lost his right arm while he helped service the pumps in the engagement of the *Bonhomme Richard*. As his boat had been of very considerable aid in saving the wounded, before the *Bonhomme Richard* had sunk, I returned his boat to him before leaving the Texel and made him a present of three complete outfits of clothes, with some linen and 100 ducats of *my own money*. Believing this pilot deserved half pay, that is, 30 livres per month, for the rest of his life, I consequently gave him a certificate to that effect, which neither France nor America has as yet honored.[50]

It is public knowledge that Admiral Rodney was detained in England for two months, because the Baltic fleet stayed during that time at Scarborough. This shows what the importance of the Baltic fleet is to the English navy. If this fleet had been captured, it is probable that Admiral Rodney would never have relieved Gibraltar.[51]

My presence and my conduct in the Texel greatly influenced the policies of the belligerent powers and contributed much toward enveloping Holland in inextricable difficulties. It is to be recalled that this was the first article of the declaration of war that England made on that republic.[52]

I was extremely appreciative of the consideration the duc de la Vauguyon showed me in Holland. This adroit ambassador rendered a most flattering account of my conduct to the minister

<hr/>

[50] Jones urged this action for several years. Jones to James Read, secretary to the agent of marine, June 23, 1783, Continental Congress Misc., Library of Congress.

[51] Admiral Rodney defeated the smaller Spanish blockading force in a night engagement off Cape St. Vincent, January 16, 1780.

[52] Britain accused the Netherlands of violating its 1678 alliance with England when it allowed "an American pirate to remain several weeks in one of their ports, and even permitted a part of his crew to mount guard in a fort in the Texel." Wharton, *Diplomatic Correspondence*, 4:220.

of the king, and conceived for me a deep attachment that will end only with life.

Because Captain Pearson of the *Serapis* conducted himself with so much bravery during the fight, I returned his sword to him before leaving the Texel, having already returned all the personal items belonging to Captain Pearson or to those who served under him that were found on board the *Serapis* and the *Countess of Scarborough*. I learned with particular pleasure that Mr. Pearson was received in England with great distinction: the king granted him the honor of knighthood, and he was given a silver service and the freedom of the towns on the east coast of England near the site of the battle.

After clearing the channel, I gained the latitude of Cape Finisterre, in the hope of taking some prizes and prisoners. I would have liked to have cruised along the coast of England, but I was unable to do so because the *Alliance* was badly equipped with sails and rigging and had only one *anchor*.

I encountered several ships but they all flew neutral flags. Finding myself at the latitude of La Corogne in Spain on January 16, 1780, I entered that port in order to procure a second anchor and to avoid a gale. After obtaining an anchor I re-turned to sea, and during my trip to Lorient I met a large American ship loaded with tobacco that I escorted to that port on February 10, 1780.

At Lorient, the repairs required by the *Alliance* were so great that she was not ready to return to sea until the middle of April, and because of the particular care I took with the repairs and the changes I had made, she had the reputation in Europe of being one of the best frigates of her time.

I loaded on the *Alliance* quantities of military stores that the king was furnishing to the United States.

At the same time, the *Serapis* arrived in Lorient from Holland and the *Countess of Scarborough* at Dunkirk. The commissioner had convinced the minister of marine to take them for the service of His Majesty without previously putting them up for auction in accordance with American maritime law. As a result the minister sent orders to Lorient to disarm the *Serapis* and to make many changes, following the ideas of the officers of the port. As a result the *Serapis* was entirely disarmed, and before I was informed of what was taking place and without my having been consulted, they destroyed all of her magazines, her parapets, her galleries, and all the interior bulkheads, as well as one bridge from stem to stern.

This was not all: the commissioner had taken charge of all the money that had come from the sale of my merchant prizes. After I had written volumes of letters to reclaim the money from the prizes and for pay and was unable to obtain satisfaction either for my officers or for the men of my crew, I presented myself at court to seek justice.

Dr. Franklin accompanied me to Versailles and the minister of marine [Sartine], upon our request, issued orders for the sale of the prizes. Although it was evident that I had suffered from the extraordinary fatigue I had undergone, having slept less than 3 hours out of every 24 during the entire campaign from Lorient to the Texel, the minister, nevertheless, received me coldly and did not even ask me if I felt any ill effects from the wounds I had received.

As a result I did not ask the minister to present me to the king, but I went with Dr. Franklin to the levee of His Majesty and the next day the prince de Beauveau, captain of the guards, did me the honor of personally presenting me to His Majesty.

At the opera, at the theater, and in all the places where I appeared, the public received me with enthusiasm and the most lively applause. This, added to the favorable reception I had from His Majesty, afforded me singular satisfaction. The minister of marine from that time on showed me marked consideration.

The comte de Maurepas informed me that His Majesty had resolved to confer on me a special mark of his royal favor and his personal esteem. This was a gold sword on which were engraved these extremely flattering words: "*Vindicati Maris Ludovicus XVI remuneratur Strenuo Vindici*" (reward from Louis XVI to the valiant avenger of the rights of the sea) with His Majesty's coat of arms, the symbols of war, and the emblems of the alliance between France and America, etc., and an important letter that His Majesty had written to Congress, proposing to confer on me the Ordre du Mérite Militaire.[53]

I was all the more anxious to find new ways of showing my gratitude for the honors that His Majesty had conferred on

---

[53] See Jones' letters to Robert Morris, June 27, 1780, and to Dumas, September 8, 1780. Wharton, *Diplomatic Correspondence*, 3:820–22, 4:48–49. Copies of Sartine's letters of May 30 and June 28, 1780, are printed in the documentary evidence section of this memoir.

48

49

me since he had never given a gold sword to any other officer and because the Ordre du Mérite Militaire had previously been given only to officers who had a commission from His Majesty.

Thus, after a conference with M. de Maurepas, I gave this minister a written plan that would in all probability have been very advantageous to the common cause of France and America if it had been executed. The considerable increase in the size of the royal navy and the high mortality rate that occurred in the combined fleet made it important for France to obtain foreign sailors. And as several frigates of the royal navy were disarmed in port, I proposed to obtain the consent of Congress and to return from America to France with the *Alliance* and the remaining frigates and with the 74-gun *America* belonging to the United States. My plan was to bring to France on this vessel and on the frigates a large enough number of American officers and men to man the frigates mentioned above and to form in this way a light squadron of 10 or 12 sail.

On this squadron, under the flag of the United States, it was proposed to embark a strong detachment of French troops drawn principally from the Irish regiments to complete the crews, and then to make raids on England and to do there what the English fleets and armies did in America. But besides the advantages that would have resulted from shore operations, this squadron would have been the surest means of intercepting the fleets from Jamaica or the Baltic and would have done more damage to the enemy than any other military force of the same expense.

M. de Maurepas, M. de Vergennes, and M. de Sartine were in agreement. In the ministerial letter written by order of His Majesty to recommend me to Congress, dated at Versailles, May 30, 1780, it was mentioned that "if Congress wished to entrust me with new expeditions in Europe, His Majesty would see me again with pleasure, and he assumed that Congress would not refuse me anything that was considered necessary to ensure the success of my enterprises."

I had intimated to M. de Sartine how flattered I would be to transport to America the portraits of Their Majesties. M. de Sartine had allowed me to hope for this honor, but as I was obliged to depart before the portraits were finished, he soothed me with the same hope upon my return. He was, however, no longer in the ministry at that time.

Because the sale of the prizes was prolonged beyond my expectation, I tried without success to obtain an advance from the minister of marine against the pay and the prize money due to my officers and men, who had lost their personal belongings when the *Bonhomme Richard* sank and were nearly naked and without money. The procedures that had been followed concerning the prizes, in the Texel and at Lorient, had raised great and dangerous clamors among the officers and men of the *Bonhomme Richard* and the *Alliance* in the Texel, and even more so at Lorient, when they saw that the *Serapis*—their property—was being torn to pieces and greatly damaged without their consent.

M. Landais, a Frenchman who had commanded the *Alliance* during the fight and who had been debarked at the Texel for his bad conduct, was then at Lorient on his way from Paris to America, to be judged there by a court-martial, and he inflamed the spirit of these Americans and persuaded them that they had served on a privateer fleet and that their only hope for justice was in America. And as Mr. Lee, recently minister of Congress, then at Lorient, joined them in this opinion for reasons known only to himself, the officers and crew of the *Alliance* mutinied against the rest of the crew of the *Bonhomme Richard* and declared they wanted to sail immediately to America under their first captain.[54]

At the same time, I had obtained from the minister of marine the loan of one of His Majesty's frigates, *l'Ariel* of 20 guns, to help the *Alliance* transport to America a quantity of military stores and clothes that the king had ordered sent to the United States. I had left 400 men on board the *Alliance*, 150 of whom I could easily have put on *l'Ariel*, but this plan was upset by the conspiracy of Mr. Lee and M. Landais, *his tool*. The officers of the *Bonhomme Richard* were greatly insulted on this occasion, and the rest of the crew of that vessel who remained faithful to me were clapped in irons on board the *Alliance*.

I had just returned to Lorient when this extraordinary event occurred. As M. Thévenard did not act with the energy required of a commanding officer in that first moment when it

---

[54] Jones' correspondence and sundry documents related to the Landais affair, including the record of the court-martial of Landais, are in PCC, item 193, fols. 1–873.

would have been easy to calm this revolt, I returned to court to obtain extraordinary authority from the minister of marine, accompanied by Mr. Franklin. As a result, the most explicit orders were issued to the officers at Lorient and at Port-Louis to detain the *Alliance* and to imprison M. Landais, *as a subject of France*, on a lettre de cachet.

They quickly prepared to detain the *Alliance* by alerting the warships and the forts and barricading the entrance to Port-Louis. But Mr. Lee advised M. Landais not to obey the king's lettre de cachet, so the affair became hopeless and M. Thévenard signed the order to fire on the *Alliance* if the frigate tried to break out of the barricaded port.

Since the English could have considered this circumstance as arising from disagreements between France and America, and because in any case these ill effects would have dishonored the American flag, I was glad to show my moderation, not being able to consent to the spilling of American or French blood in order to give myself a command. Therefore, I begged M. Thévenard to retract his orders and open the entrance to the port, which was done, and the *Alliance* departed for America.

M. Thévenard assembled the principal officers, who signed a statement outlining the preparations that had been made to detain the *Alliance*, and who expressed their admiration for my conduct.[55]

I have already reported that I had lost all of my personal belongings when the *Bonhomme Richard* sank, and it can be said that the revolt on the *Alliance* caused me to suffer about the same misfortunes.

Mr. Lee embarked on this frigate for America and during the voyage he formulated a second conspiracy that he executed by removing from command M. Landais, who was arrested and brought to Boston as a prisoner. There a court-martial was convened, which cashiered this ill-advised man and dishonorably discharged him from the service for having seized command of the *Alliance* at Lorient. If he had been judged on his conduct while he was under my command, the charges against him would

---

[55] The correspondence of Thévenard shows a more direct participation of the French ministry in this affair. Lettres du ministre, Service historique de la marine, Archives du port de Lorient, Series I, E4.

have been of a nature to have put his life in danger. It was proved in M. Landais' trial that Mr. Lee had put *merchandise* on board the *Alliance* that he would not have been able to embark under my command.

The minister of marine then gave orders for the complete rearming and refitting of *l'Ariel*. Only 45 men and officers from the crew of the *Bonhomme Richard* remained with me because the rest had been put in irons on board the *Alliance* until they reached America, without having received their pay or their share of the prizes. The 45 men were the only ones who were finally paid their salaries, after great difficulty, but not their shares in the *prizes*.

The *Serapis*, which had cost the English government 50,000 guineas six months before it was captured, was after a long delay sold to the king for 240,000 livres, one-fifth of what it had cost, which can only be attributed to the disarmament of this beautiful vessel and the destruction of the decks, magazines, etc., in accordance with the orders the minister had given before the sale.

My position at Lorient on *l'Ariel*, which had but 20 cannon, while the *Serapis* which I had captured was put under the command of a man who had done nothing to merit this honor, was a subject of reflection that did not escape men of good sense, and it was generally said *"that having killed the Lion, I deserved the skin."*

M. de Maurepas, however, did not forget the arrangements he had made with me for my return from America to Europe. This minister wrote me a letter, dated August 23, 1780, giving full approval to this plan and promising all the facilities that the government could provide to ensure its execution.[56]

After *l'Ariel* was armed and ready to put to sea, I was detained for some time by contrary winds and storms. I left October 8, 1780, with a favorable wind; but the following night the wind became contrary, and I was driven by a furious storm close to the rocks of Penmark between Brest and Lorient. The storm became so violent that *l'Ariel* could not carry sail, and

---

[56] This letter is printed under the date August 15, 1780, in the documentary evidence section of this memoir. Jones' stay in Lorient as commander of *L'Ariel* is detailed in Barnes, *The Logs of the Serapis—Alliance—Ariel*, pp. 91–119.

not having enough room to run before the wind, she was nearly capsized. There was so much water in the hold that the pumps no longer sufficed.

Since the depth of the water rapidly diminished and there was no hope of saving ourselves if l'Ariel struck against the rocks, which are a considerable distance from land, I dropped anchor as a last resort. But after playing out 200 fathoms of cable I was unable to head the frigate into the wind, and the ends of the main yards to leeward touched the water from time to time. As a result, I had no choice but to cut down the foremast. This produced the desired effects and l'Ariel immediately came into the wind. But the heel of the mainmast would not stay in place and its movement could be compared to that of an unsteady drunkard.

Because there was great danger that it would break below deck or drive a hole in the bottom of the frigate, I had it cut down, and in falling it brought down the mizzenmast and the bridge.

In this condition l'Ariel held her anchor in open sea, in the wind, and on the edge of the most dangerous rocks in the world, for two days and three nights, in a tempest that covered the shores with wrecks and even endangered vessels moored in the port of Lorient. It is to be presumed that never before had a vessel been saved in such circumstances.

After the storm I had jury masts rigged and I returned to Lorient and wrote to M. de Castries, who had then become minister of marine, from there to ask him to exchange l'Ariel for the frigate Terpsicore, which I did not obtain. I was therefore detained in Lorient to remast l'Ariel until December 18, 1780, and then put to sea for Philadelphia. As I was entrusted with the court's dispatches for the past six months for the chevalier de la Luzerne, the French fleet, and the army which was in America, I did not want to encounter the enemy during my passage. I could foresee purposes of much greater importance, namely, to obtain the approbation of Congress for my past conduct and to be returned to France in order to execute the plan that M. de Maurepas had approved.

But after many encounters, I finally fell in with a frigate of 20 guns belonging to the English navy and called the Triumph.

As this frigate sailed at much greater speed than l'Ariel, I was unable to avoid an encounter, but I maneuvered sails and rudder in such a manner, and I hid all the preparations for combat so well, that the enemy had no other thoughts than those of an easy conquest and a good prize.

At nightfall the *Triumph* steered within hailing distance of *l'Ariel* and the enemy were not a little surprised to find that they were up against forces equal to their own. As the two frigates were then flying the English flag, the captain [John Pindar] of the *Triumph* and I began a conversation from which I learned the exact state of English affairs in America. Finally I pretended to believe that the *Triumph* did not belong to the English navy, and I insisted that her captain come aboard to show me his commission. The captain excused himself, complaining that his boats were leaking and that I had told him neither my name nor the name of my frigate. I answered that I did not have to account to him, and that I would give him five minutes to decide. The time elapsed and *l'Ariel* being situated directly in front of and to the leeward of the *Triumph*, some 30 feet away, I hauled up the American flag and commenced firing. In earlier combats I had never felt so satisfied as I did during this one with the regular and vigorous firing from the rigging and the batteries of *l'Ariel*. This resulted from plans and preparations made before the action by stationing passengers and the officers of *l'Ariel* everywhere to stop men from abandoning their posts and to encourage everyone to do his duty, which demonstrates the great advantage of having several good officers. For never was there a crew worse than that of *l'Ariel*.

After a brief resistance, the enemy lowered their flag. The captain of the *Triumph* asked for quarter, saying that he surrendered and that half of his crew were dead. As a result I ceased fire, and as usual after a victory there were many *huzzahs* and cries of joy on *l'Ariel*. But a minute later the captain of the *Triumph* deceitfully set sail and fled. It was not in my power to prevent his flight, the enemy frigate being much faster than *l'Ariel*. But if the English government had possessed the sentiments of honor and justice that become a great nation, they would have delivered this frigate to the United States as their property and punished the captain in an exemplary manner for having thus violated the laws of war and the practices of civilized nations.

The enemy had been advised of my approach by the accident that had forced *l'Ariel* to return to France after being dismasted, and two English frigates had been stationed at the entrance of the Delaware to intercept me. But the two frigates had taken several valuable prizes and were escorting them to New York, and during their absence I arrived safely at Philadelphia.[57]

The chevalier de la Luzerne informed Congress "that His Majesty had honored me with a gold sword and proposed to decorate me with the Ordre Royal du Mérite Militaire; which would be, His Majesty presumed, considered by both sides *as one more tie between the two nations, etc.*" As a result Congress postponed the general confederation of the United States for three days, in order first to pass a law authorizing me to be decorated with the Ordre du Mérite Militaire; this took place on February 27, 1781.[58] Congress instructed the minister plenipotentiary of the United States to the court of France to inform His Most Christian Majesty of the great satisfaction "that Congress had received from the court of France by the letter of M. de Sartine, dated May 30, 1780, in which that minister expressed the esteem and approval that His Majesty granted to my good conduct and my bravery in Europe and that the offer of His Majesty to award me his Ordre du Mérite Militaire could only be infinitely agreeable to Congress."

Consequently, the chevalier de la Luzerne gave a reception for all the members of Congress and the leading citizens of Philadelphia, and in their presence he invested me, in the name of His Majesty, with the Ordre du Mérite Militaire.

The animosity that unfortunately prevailed among the three American ministers plenipotentiary at Paris had naturally produced contradictions in their reports concerning American affairs in Europe, and some people, who did not at all understand on what basis I had remained there for so long, had propagated in America their opinion that I was in Europe only to command a fleet of privateers. As a result, Congress ordered the Admiralty

---

[57] George Washington reported on the sailing of six ships from New York, including the 74-gun *Russel*, which Washington believed might head for the Delaware to cut off Jones' squadron. Washington to the vicomte de la Touche, May 19, 1780. Washington, *Writings* (Fitzpatrick), 18:393–94.

[58] Jones obtained his authorization two days before the Maryland members of Congress ratified the Articles of Confederation. Morison, *Jones*, p. 310; JCC, 19:175–76, 200.

to examine closely my relationship with the court of France and the reasons for the detention in Europe of clothes and military stores that belonged to the United States.[59] The Admiralty posed a great number of questions to me by letter. To answer them, I entered into an explanation of all my conduct from the beginning of the war, and I revealed the details of my connections with the court and the reasons (insofar as I knew them) that had delayed delivery of the provisions of war and the clothes that had been prepared in Europe for the army of General Washington. I documented my responses with more than 100 pieces of original or copied official letters.[60]

This examination was followed by a report from the Admiralty to Congress, infinitely honorable for me, and one of the members proposed this question: "*What shall we do for the man whom the king is pleased to honor?*"

After this report from the Admiralty Council, Congress named a committee of three members to examine the measures and proceedings on which this report was based, and as a result of the account that was submitted by the committee, Congress passed an act on April 14, 1781, in which it approved and highly lauded my conduct and honored me with the most flattering thanks "for the zeal, the prudence, and the intrepidity, with which I had sustained the honor of the American flag; for my bold and dexterous enterprises designed to redeem from captivity the American citizens who had fallen into the power of England, and in general for my good conduct and the eminent services by which I added luster to my own character and to American arms."[61] The committee was also

---

[59] The delegates generally were disappointed by Jones' failure to bring uniforms from France. Jones' arrival "would have been a much more pleasing one had he brought the cloathing so long and anxiously expected. His Cargo is however by no means useless as it Consists of about thirty Ton of Powder." Virginia delegates to Gov. Thomas Jefferson, February [20], 1781, Edmund C. Burnett, ed., *Letters of Members of the Continental Congress*, 8 vols. (Washington: Carnegie Institution of Washington, 1921–36), 5:577. Jones did make time and space to bring John Adams' consignment of goods intended for his wife, Abigail, and several friends in Massachusetts. See James Lovell to Abigail Adams, February 27, 1781, Lyman H. Butterfield and Marc Friedlaender, eds., *Adams Family Correspondence* (Cambridge: Belknap Press of Harvard University Press, 1963–), 4:81–83n.

[60] See PCC, items 168 and 193.

[61] The Board of Admiralty reported on March 28, 1781, that it had interrogated Jones regarding "the causes of the cloathing and military stores not being exported." The board absolved Jones of all blame for the delay and placed the responsibility on "the malconduct of Mr. Landais." Jones faithfully reported the congressional resolves, but the editor noted: "At the end of the report is written by some one not on the committee: 'God send it to be true.'" JCC, 19:318–20, 390–91n.

of the opinion *that I deserved a gold medal that would attest to the good wishes and thanks I had received.*

At the time I had given my plan to M. de Maurepas to form a combined squadron under the American flag to be manned by officers and sailors from the United States and by troops detached from French regiments, Congress possessed the following naval force, beside a number of smaller armed vessels, namely:

Alliance	*36*	*cannons*
Confederation	*36*	”
Warren	*32*	”
Raleigh	*32*	”
Providence	*32*	”
Trumbull	*32*	”
Boston	*30*	”
Deane	*30*	”
Queen of France	*20*	”
Ranger	*18*	”
Saratoga	*18*	”

And according to the most recent intelligence, it appeared then that the *America*, a new ship of 74 guns, was also ready for service.

It is therefore certain that half of these frigates, with the ship *America*, would have sufficed to transport their own crews from America to France, plus a sufficient number of officers and sailors for the manning of the frigates that M. de Maurepas had agreed to put under my command, and that there was every reason to believe Congress would adopt this plan.

But in the long interval of the delay I experienced in France after having given my plan to the minister and the voyage that I next made between France and America, the maritime forces of Congress had greatly diminished. The enemy had cap- tured five frigates at Penobscot and Charleston, two others had been taken at sea, one had been driven ashore and seized, and one other was burned or lost in the breakers. So there remained only the *Alliance* of 36 guns, the *Deane* of 30 guns, and the *America* of 74 guns, which was still in the stocks in Portsmouth, N.H.

It is easy to see from these disastrous circumstances that it was not in the power of Congress to support the views of the court of France by sending me immediately back to France with the force of men and vessels that had been proposed. Congress, however, did not lose sight of this plan and on June 26, 1781, it unanimously chose me as commander of the 74-gun *America*. There had been talk of raising me to the rank of rear admiral, but this proposal was not supported by my friends in Congress because the United States did not then have sufficient forces for an officer of that rank.[62] In these circumstances I returned *l'Ariel* to the chevalier de la Luzerne. It was believed in Philadelphia that the *America* was so far advanced that she would be able to set sail for France by the beginning of winter, and the Congress then proposed to put under my orders the other frigates, that is to say, the *Alliance* of 36 guns, the *Deane* of 30 guns, and a new frigate called the *Bourbon*, then on the stocks in Connecticut.

Now is the time to mention what happened on October 10, 1776, that is to say, three months after independence was declared. Congress made a new list of naval officers, in which all the brave officers who had generously exposed themselves at sea for the American cause and had captured New Providence found themselves preceded on the seniority list by newly appointed officers, who had not yet been in the service of Congress. If in this new list preference had been given only to men of superior and recognized ability, something could be said in favor of that choice; but this was not the case. Far from having merited preference, those who obtained it were without military experience. Exaggerating the dangers, they found pretexts not to embark on the first squadron, and they did not offer their services to Congress until after the question of independence was raised. It is fair to add that throughout the Revolution none of them so distinguished himself as to merit the preference he had received. Although during the useful and glorious expedition to *New Providence*, I received early recognition of my faithful service; and although after that I gave further proof of my zeal, and on August 8, 1776, I received from the president of Congress the first captain's commission granted in the

---

[62] Jones was apparently considered for the rank of rear admiral, but the opposition claims of Thomas Read and James Nicholson, senior captains in the United States Navy, caused the move to be tabled. Morison, *Jones*, pp. 315–16; *JCC*, 20:572, 590, 698, 710–11. For the letters and memorials of Jones, Read, and Nicholson, see PCC, item 41, 7:67–70, 8:306–7; item 168, 1:474–76.

United States Navy, immediately after the Declaration of Independence; nevertheless, because of the arrangement of
October 10, 1776, I saw 13 individuals pass ahead of me, none of
whom had embarked from the commencement of hostilities.
Such an affront could not have happened to officers in a well
organized service; if it had occurred, the officers would have
inevitably resigned their commissions to save their honor. But
I saw this matter from a different point of view. I was not
fighting for seniority. My ambition concerned freedom for
America, and I was willing to make the greatest sacrifices
for this cause: thus I considered myself less as an officer of
Congress than as a man fighting for the cause of *mankind*.
And I was persuaded that one day Congress would render me
justice in regard to seniority, and it was in fact accorded me by
the unanimous vote of that honorable body on June 26, 1781.[63]

Upon my arrival at Portsmouth, N.H., I found myself
involved in problems that neither my friends nor I had foreseen
in Philadelphia. Instead of being ready to launch, the *America*
was not half constructed, and there was neither wood, nor iron,
nor other material prepared to finish the job. Even if there had
been an abundance of money, and if it had been well employed,
it would have been impossible to procure the men or the necessary materials to complete and launch the *America* in twice the
time that had been proposed. But money was lacking. The Admiralty at Boston had used the funds which the finance minister
had designated for the *America* for other purposes.

The construction of this vessel, which had been delayed for
a year, was, however, immediately resumed and some progress
was made before winter. In the course of that season the masts
and the construction wood were prepared, and during the
spring and summer the *America* was completed.

The most disagreeable service to which I was assigned
during the whole course of the Revolution was to supervise the
slow construction of this ship. But from start to finish, I never

---

[63] Congress appointed Jones to the command of the *America* on that day. JCC, 20:698.
A committee of Congress on June 29, 1781, reported that the captain's list of October 10, 1776,
was of dubious arrangement. "The Committee cannot fully ascertain the rule by which the
arrangement was made, as the relative rank was not conformable to time of appointment or
dates of commission and seems repugnant to a resolution of Congress of 22nd of December A.D.
1775." JCC, 20:710–11. The political aspects of the appointment of naval officers are discussed
in Morison, *Jones*, pp. 88–91.

lost sight of my plan for forming a combined squadron of French and American frigates, supported by the *America*.

The enemy formulated several plans for the destruction of this vessel, and I was so informed by spies from *New York*, who also sent reports to General Washington and to Philadelphia. But despite my pleas for aid from the government of *New Hampshire* to guard and defend the *America*, I was not able to obtain a single soldier. I had, moreover, neither arms, nor powder, nor bullets, and there was not any way I could remedy this unless I procured the aid with my own money. So this is what I did. I also engaged two shipwrights to guard the ship alternately every night, with a party of carpenters that I also hired at my own expense. Since it was necessary to set an example, I took command of the guard every third night for the duration of the construction. By these measures the enemy was prevented from burning the *America*, although several times large boats with muffled oars entered the river for this purpose; but they did not dare come alongside after they learned that the watch duty was performed so carefully.

In the month of June 1782, the chevalier de la Luzerne received orders from the court of France to announce to Congress the birth of a dauphin, and the Congress issued orders for public rejoining on this occasion.

Since the *America* was not yet armed, I was not included in the orders that were given by Congress for the celebration of the birth of the dauphin. But I would have felt too much regret if I had allowed an occasion which gave such joy to Their Majesties, and in which I sincerely shared, to pass by without any honors. I therefore put the necessary artillery on board the *America* and purchased with my money the powder and everything else that was needed for this celebration, held in the following manner.

> Description of the festivities by which Commodore Paul Jones, in the month of June 1782, celebrated at his own expense (on board the *America* of 74 guns and at Portsmouth, capital of New Hampshire) the birth of Monseigneur le Dauphin.

At sunrise the *America*, decorated with the colors of Congress and with the French flag being hoisted up forward, gave a 21-gun royal salute, to which all the forts responded.

At noon the same salute was repeated by the *America* and the forts. This was the signal for all the citizens to come take part in an elegant feast prepared for them at the townhall of Portsmouth. During the meal, according to the custom of the country, 13 toasts were made to honor Their Majesties and the dauphin. At each of the toasts the *America*, alerted by a signal from the townhall, fired a royal salute, and all day until midnight she kept up a rolling fire of muskets and pistols.

As soon as it was dark, the *America* was decorated with brilliant lights, by means of huge lanterns that were designed for this occasion and placed all over the ship; when they were illuminated, fireworks commenced that lasted until midnight. The night was very dark, which contributed greatly toward giving maximum luster to the illuminations and the fireworks. The entire celebration so excited public curiosity that all the inhabitants of the city and the surrounding area assembled on the shore of the river and showed their admiration by their applause.

The close came at midnight with the firing of a royal salute by the *America*.

As a result, I had the honor to receive from the chevalier de la Luzerne a very flattering letter dated from Philadelphia, July 29, 1782. However, there is reason to believe that the celebration I had at Portsmouth at *my own expense* was confused with those Congress had ordered and paid for.[64]

The *America* was 50 feet 6 inches at her beam and 182 feet 6 inches long at her first gundeck, according to English measurements. Though this vessel of 74 guns was the largest of her class, because of the manner in which I had directed her construction the *America* appeared to be no other than an elegant frigate, and when the gunports of the lower battery were closed, a stranger at a distance of a mile would not have believed he was approaching a ship of the line. The work was completed so well that it greatly surpassed all that naval architecture had previously offered; and all that Abbé Raynal needed was to have seen this ship to have given the world a more grandiose idea of the continent for which it was named. It was no less true than astonishing that only 20 men were employed in the construction of this entire ship, despite the dif-

---

[64] This letter is printed in the documentary evidence section of this memoir.

ficulties occasioned by the ponderous proportions of some of its parts. Several of the *principal beams* used in the first deck were hewn from single trees. I could not, however, answer for the expected lifetime of every piece used in this ship, because time had been too short to prepare each piece properly, and during the final stages of construction circumstances would not permit all the care one would have desired in the choice of masts. But it is certain that His Majesty could find good construction wood and masts more easily in America than in any other country.

An unfortunate accident deprived me of the command of this beautiful ship, the *America*, after all the time, all the effort, and all the personal expense that its construction had cost me. *Le Magnifique*, a 74-gun ship from the marquis de Vaudreuil's fleet, was lost off Boston, and Congress seized this occasion to prove its gratitude to His Most Christian Majesty by voting on September 3, 1782, to present the *America* to His Majesty as a replacement for *le Magnifique*. She remained under my command until November 5, and then I delivered this ship to the chevalier de Martigne, who had commanded *le Magnifique* and whom the marquis de Vaudreuil had sent to Portsmouth to assume command of the *America*.[65]

Immediately thereafter I went from Portsmouth to Philadelphia. After I had left the Texel, *l'Indienne*, the frigate of which I have spoken several times in these memoirs, had been lent by His Most Christian Majesty to the prince of Luxembourg for three years, and the prince of Luxembourg had leased it for a profit to an officer in the service of South Carolina.[66] *L'Indienne*, after many delays, had consequently set sail to leave the waters of Holland and was at present in Philadelphia, having done nothing for the state of South Carolina but bring it heavy expenses. And as the chevalier de la Luzerne had been empowered by the prince of Luxembourg to claim payment for the lease of *l'Indienne*, and to take possession of that

---

[65] For a discussion of the building of the *America* see Lawrence S. Mayo, *John Langdon of New Hampshire* (Concord, N.H.: Rumford Press, 1937), pp. 175–76; and Robert W. Neeser, "The True Story of the *America*," *United States Naval Institute Proceedings* 34 (1908):573–80. For the action of Congress, see *JCC*, 23:543.

[66] The duc de Montmorency Luxembourg was her owner. Alexander Gillon commanded her as the *South Carolina* for that state. Lorenz, *Jones*, p. 500.

ship and dispose of it at the expiration of the lease, which was nearly terminated, he consulted with Mr. Morris, minister of finance. They decided to give me command of *l'Indienne*, along with two or three other frigates and some troops, with orders to capture the Island of *Bermuda*. But despite the measures taken to carry out this plan, it failed, and *l'Indienne* sailed out and was captured without resistance by a much inferior force.

As I foresaw that the plan conceived by the chevalier de la Luzerne and Mr. Morris would probably not be carried out, I addressed myself to Congress without losing any time, and on December 4, 1782, I obtained an act from that body ordering me to embark on a ship of His Majesty's fleet at Boston, under the orders of the marquis de Vaudreuil, scheduled to join the comte d'Estaing in his expedition against Jamaica, etc.[67]

The prospect was very agreeable to me, because of all those who were assigned to serve on this expedition no one knew the Island of Jamaica as well as I, and since the comte d'Estaing had commanded a fleet of more than 70 ships of the line and a great army, I hoped to find myself in the best military school in the world, where I would be able to render myself very useful and would necessarily acquire very important knowledge about conducting large-scale military operations.

The marquis de Vaudreuil received me politely on board his own flagship, *le Triomphant*, and billeted me in the Council Chamber with the baron de Viomenil, who commanded the land forces. The marquis de Vaudreuil's squadron of 10 ships of the line, two frigates, and one cutter left Boston on December 24. The admiral's intention was to join at the latitude of Portsmouth with two other ships of the line, *l'Auguste* and *le Pluton*, then in that port and under the orders of his brother (as the *America* was still not ready to put to sea); but stormy weather and contrary winds prevented this juncture and put the squadron into a disagreeable situation because of the proximity of the coast and of the Bay of Fundy. The admiral then attempted to join the ship *le Fantasque*, carrying troops from Rhode Island, but this also failed. The squadron, having lost sight of several ships loaded with masts and 20 merchant-

---

[67] See JCC, 23:758–59, 761.

men being convoyed to Boston, set course for the Island of Puerto Rico.

When that island was within sight, the marquis de Vaudreuil was warned that Admiral Hood was cruising at the latitude of Cape François with 16 vessels of the line, and that Admiral Pigot, with greater forces, was at Saint Lucia, so that the enemy would necessarily consider the marquis de Vaudreuil's squadron an easy prey that could not escape Hood or Pigot.

The marquis de Vaudreuil remained at the latitude of San Juan, Island of Puerto Rico, for 10 days, practiced all kinds of fleet maneuvers, and then took 16 ships from a large convoy that had arrived at San Juan from France and headed toward the western end of Puerto Rico.

Some of the flyboats sent to cruise by Hood perceived the squadron near the Mona Passage and immediately went to inform him that the marquis de Vaudreuil was sailing south of St. Domingue on the way to some port on the west coast of that island or on the east side of Cuba, for the expedition to Jamaica. They were in error: the squadron headed south, into the wind, and passed to the leeward and within sight of the Island of Curaçao, near the South American coast.

The rendezvous that had been agreed upon by Don Solano and the marquis de Vaudreuil at Cape François after the defeat of the comte de Grasse was held in utmost secrecy, and no one had the least idea that it was Porto Cabello on the continent of South America at 20 leagues to the windward of Curaçao. The squadron maneuvered for three weeks along the coast against a current that chased the transport ships out of sight to the leeward; and because they had neither pilots nor good charts of this coast on board the squadron, la Bourgogne of 74 guns foundered on rocks at night two leagues from the coast and went down with 200 men, including officers, among them the first lieutenant. Le Triomphant arrived at Porto Cabello on February 18, 1783. L'Auguste and le Pluton had arrived there some days before and the other ships of the fleet came in safely, one after the other.

Don Solano had planned to meet with the marquis de Vaudreuil at Porto Cabello in December. He did not keep his promise, and no news of his squadron was received at Porto Cabello. The anxiety that this uncertainty occasioned, combined with the lack of news from Europe, so deeply affected the spirit of several officers that they fell ill, and I myself was dangerously sick.

Finally the news of a general peace arrived by frigate from France. The most brilliant successes and the most in-structive experience in the art of war could not have given me pleasure comparable to that which I felt when I learned that Great Britain, after such a long struggle, had been forced to recognize the sovereignty and independence of the United States of America.

On April 8, 1783, the day after the cessation of hostilities, the squadron left Porto Cabello, and after a voyage of eight days it arrived safely at Cape François.

The Spanish squadron had left Havanna for Porto Cabello, and upon receiving news of the peace at Puerto Rico it changed course for Cape François and arrived there a few days before the marquis de Vaudreuil.

I remained only a short time at Cape François where I received the special favors of M. de Bellecombe, the governor. I then embarked for Philadelphia, filled with gratitude for all the attention I had received from the marquis de Vaudreuil, the baron de Viomenil, and the other officers during the five months that I had been on board His Majesty's squadron.[68]

I was not able to regain my health during the remainder of the summer in Pennsylvania; I recovered it only in autumn, with the aid of cold baths.[69]

I then addressed myself to Congress to be authorized to return to Europe to settle the claims of the officers and men who had served on the squadron I had commanded in Europe with the court of France. And Congress so authorized me by an act dated at Prince-town on November 1, 1783.

In the arrangement of this affair, I wanted to take effective measures to prevent even the possibility of any reproach, and therefore I gave the minister of finance bond for 200,000 Rixdaller that he was to transfer to the Treasury of Congress, proportionately to the sums of money belonging to the citizens of the United States that I would recuperate, so the

---

[68] Morison described Jones' activities with the French fleet in *Jones*, pp. 331–33.

[69] Jones spent most of the summer at the Moravian sanatorium in Bethlehem, Pa., where he took their cold bath treatment. Morison, *Jones*, p. 333.

minister could pay individuals from the Treasury, hoping to prove by this that I had nothing to gain personally.

I embarked at Philadelphia November 10 in a small packet boat bound for Havre-de-Grace.[70] Because this ship was very old and damp, I did not want to risk taking the sword with which His Most Christian Majesty had honored me, so I left it at Philadelphia.

The packet boat was forced by contrary winds to enter at Plymouth, and as I was entrusted with public dispatches of importance I immediately took the mail carriage for London and was so diligent that five days after my departure from Plymouth I reached Paris and delivered my dispatches.

The maréchal de Castries and the comte de Vergennes received me with great politeness, and when I gave them the letters of the chevalier de la Luzerne, which told them of the commission with which I was entrusted and in which he pointed out several things that were favorable to me, both assured me that I had no need of any recommendations to convince them to do me justice or to ensure me of their esteem.

The maréchal de Castries did me the honor of presenting me to the king on December 20, 1783, and after dinner this minister took me aside and told me on behalf of the king "that His Majesty had been pleased to see me again, and would always be glad to further my interests."

The commissioner had taken possession of all money produced by the sale of the Countess of Scarborough and the merchant vessels and had retained it for more than four years without rendering an account to the captors on either the principal or the interest. He wanted to keep the prize money because the king, he said, owed him 109,179 livres, 15 sols, 4 deniers.

As soon as I informed the maréchal de Castries of this, he withdrew the papers concerning the prizes from the commissioner and gave them to M. Chardon, maître des requêtes.[71]

On February 10, 1784, the maréchal de Castries sent me M. Chardon's report on the liquidation of the prizes, after that affair had passed from the commissioner's hands into his own,

---

[70] Jones sailed on the ship *Washington*, formerly the *General Monk* of Great Britain.
[71] The judge of claims under the duc de Penthièvre, grand admiral of France. Morison, *Jones*, pp. 338–39.

in order for me to inspect it. By this statement of settlement, the commissioner had evaluated all of the prizes at only 456,787 livres, 2 sols, 9 deniers, and he listed expenses so high that the result for the captors was a balance of only 283,631 livres, 13 sols.

Six months before the capture of the *Serapis*, it had cost the government of Great Britain 50,000 guineas and the *Countess of Scarborough* has cost them 22,000, which was in all 1,728,000 livres, but according to the liquidations of the commissioner the captors were credited for the *Serapis* only 96,875 livres, 2 sols, 2 deniers and for the *Countess of Scarborough* 59,198 livres, 5 sols, 9 deniers, which made for the two warships only 156,073 livres, 7 sols, 11 deniers.[72]

On February 18, 1784, I sent the maréchal de Castries my observations on the work that M. Chardon had done for the settlement of the prizes pursuant to what had been proposed by the commissioner, showing again that when I entered the Texel in accordance with definitive orders, I was obliged by indispensable necessity to take with me the *Serapis* and the *Countess of Scarborough*, because the *Alliance* and *la Pallas* had neither enough water nor provisions and could not hold the remainder of the crew of the *Bonhomme Richard* along with the prisoners of war that numbered nearly 600.

As the great number of prisoners had been the main reason that prevented my ordering the *Serapis* and the *Countess of Scarborough* to head for America a day or two after being captured, and while the attention of the British navy was still fixed on the combined fleet in the channel and on the one commanded by the comte d'Estaing off the coast of America, it seemed unjust to me to charge the captors with any of the expenses incurred in Holland in regard to the two prizes. And it is impossible to find a single example that could justify the commissioner in having thus charged the captors for the expenses of provisions consumed by the crews of those vessels and *by their prisoners of war.*

If these two warships had been sent to America instead of entering the Texel, they would have been subject only to

[72] Documents related to the settlement of the prize cases can be seen in the Jones Papers; Lettres du ministère, Archives du port de Lorient, Series 2P50 and 2P69; and Bibliothèque historique de la marine, Series CC 1247. Dossier personnels, John Paul Jones. All are on microfilm at the Library of Congress.

their will, being the property of the captors according to the laws of Congress. And it is to be presumed that these two prizes would have been sold in America without additional expense to the captors beyond their agent's commission and for at least 30 percent above what they had cost the government of Britain.

Instead of that, the *Serapis* and the *Countess of Scarborough* remained in the Texel as prison ships for more than three months, and then they were brought to France *at the risk of their captors*, although they were not under their command, during the entire route and in the face of all of the ships England had sent out to intercept them.

When the *Serapis* had arrived at Lorient, the commissioner obtained orders from M. de Sartine, in conformity with the intention of Mr. Franklin, *according to what he claimed*, to destroy an entire deck and the interior to make changes. This damage was done without the consent of the captors and without their knowledge. And the *Serapis* was so degraded that it was finally sold to the king for one-fifth of what it had cost England shortly before it was captured.

But what affected me more deeply than all the other circumstances in which I was involved during the American Revolution was a letter that I received from Mr. Franklin, dated at Passy, March 25, 1784,[73] in which this minister plenipotentiary, speaking of the prisoners taken by the squadron and brought to Holland, said: "Not a one of them was exchanged for Americans in England, in accordance with your intention, and *as we both had been led to hope*."

The higher men are, the more their promises should be sacred. I had always counted to the utmost on those M. de Sartine had made me in the beginning of our relationship and particularly on this one: "that the prisoners taken by the squadron, will be exchanged for Americans in England." This was all the reward I had asked for my services, and I had spent many days in anxiety and many nights without sleep in the hope of liberating unfortunate American prisoners in England.

In the month of June 1784, I had personal reasons and affairs that absolutely demanded my return to America. M.

---

[73] This letter is printed in the documentary evidence section of this memoir.

Chardon had finished the settlement of the prizes and the maréchal de Castries promised me a signed statement from him in time for me to embark with the marquis de Lafayette. As a result I prepared for this voyage, but the delays occurring in the bureau made me lose not only this opportunity, but the entire summer; and I did not obtain the statement of settlement of my prizes, signed by the maréchal de Castries, until October 23, 1784. By then my journey to America had been delayed too long and would no longer be of any use for the projects that had motivated it.

From the beginning of the alliance between France and America, I had resolved to place before the eyes of the minister of marine a plan to furnish the French navy with all kinds of construction wood, masts, tar, etc., from America. In the month of June 1784, I had the honor to present to the maréchal de Castries the first plan that had been produced for this purpose, showing the great advantages that would result for the commerce of both nations, as well as for the royal navy of France. The comte de Vergennes and M. de Calonne, to whom I also addressed my plan, received it in a most favorable manner, and the maréchal de Castries told me that the information he had obtained in connection with my plan had convinced him to send a shipwright to America to examine the wood before acting on the contract.

Although the maréchal de Castries had signed the statement of settlement for my prizes on October 23, 1784, I was nevertheless forced to wait until the end of July 1785 before being able to obtain orders authorizing payment. I was then obliged to make a trip to Lorient where I was detained until September 5, 1785, before receiving from Paris the letters of credit necessary to divide the prize money that by the final settlement was due to the Americans on the crews of the *Bonhomme Richard* and to the crew of the *Alliance*. By this final settlement the captors were authorized to receive for the *Serapis* and the *Countess of Scarborough* the sum of 257,085 livres, 2 sols, 6 deniers, which was a little more than *one-seventh* of what these prizes had cost England before they had been captured. The reason was that the captors were charged for the expenses of their prizes both in Holland and in France, and that they were granted nothing for their three months' service in the Texel as prison ships, nor were they compensated for the degradation inflicted on the *Serapis* at Lorient by order of M. de Sartine before she was sold.

The officers of the *Bonhomme Richard*, who, after the mutiny on board the *Alliance* in the port of Lorient, had been brought in irons on that frigate from France to America, still had a claim to 20,548 livres, 9 sols, 8 deniers representing their salaries for which I found myself responsible by the terms of the contract I had signed with them, and which I will be unable to satisfy until this sum is paid to me out of navy funds.

During the course of the war I had never found a means of returning to the countess of Selkirk the family plate I had been obliged to allow my men to take at the time of my Scottish expedition on the *Ranger*. I had purchased this plate at a very high price from my men; they thought they could not make me pay too much for it. I had planned to send it from Lorient by sea, when that place became a free port; but, unable to find the opportunity, I wrote the comte de Vergennes to obtain permission to ship this plate from Lorient to Calais by land. This minister considered my letter and sent it to M. de Calonne, who not only granted me the permission I had requested but wrote a flattering letter to me on this occasion. As a result the plate was transported to London and deposited there in the name of Count Selkirk, free of all cost or expense. I received from this lord a letter full of gratitude for the delicacy of my conduct and the strict discipline of my men.

It was noted at the proper time that M. de Sartine had promised to place 500 men from the Régiment Irlandais de Walsh on the squadron I commanded. However, this embarkation never occurred; but the officers of that regiment manifested their lively desire to serve with me, and three junior lieutenants obtained permission from the court to do so. One of them [Lt. James Gerard O'Kelly] was killed in the engagement between the *Bonhomme Richard* and the *Serapis*. The other two received orders at the Texel to rejoin their regiment then embarking for the West Indies. I gave them testimonials of good conduct, particularly during the engagement with the *Serapis*, when one of them (Mr. Stack) commanded a party in the mainmast riggings, and the other (Mr. MacCarthy) had been slightly wounded in the powder magazine where the cannons exploded.

By presenting my certificates to the minister of war on December 12, 1779, they were immediately promoted from junior lieutenants to captains, and they received a monetary award for the loss of their belongings when the *Bonhomme Richard* sank after the battle. I was deeply moved by the credit placed on the recommendations I had given, and I am sincerely flattered to learn that on February 17, 1785, His Majesty in his bounty awarded Mr. Stack an annual pension of 400 livres and that the following April 10 he deigned to do the same for Mr. MacCarthy, and that these two pensions had been awarded for their good conduct on board the *Bonhomme Richard*. In addition the comte d'Estaing, the marquis de Lafayette, and the marquis de Saint Simon had joined their recommendations to mine in order to obtain the privilege for Mr. Stack and Mr. MacCarthy to be decorated with the Order of the Cincinnati.[74]

These two young officers merited the rewards they received for their services on board the *Bonhomme Richard;* but because they left the squadron in the Texel, their service was of short duration in comparison to the other officers who served under my orders. And even in this battle several junior officers of the *Bonhomme Richard* were more meritorious than they and yet received nothing for their bravery, not even indemnity for the loss of their personal belongings when the sea swallowed the *Bonhomme Richard*.

Although I felt obliged, during the American Revolution, to refuse a commission in the navy of His Majesty, nevertheless I presume that I could be considered as having been in the service of His Majesty from February 10, 1778, the time when I presented my plan for the first expedition in America, which was commanded by the comte d'Estaing, or at least from the following June 1, when Dr. Franklin informed me at Brest that His Majesty wanted me to journey to Versailles. And although in the realization of my projects I have been sometimes countered by various circumstances, I dare flatter myself that His Majesty is convinced that my zeal was never dimmed by all the obstacles I had to surmount.

It is true that after my return to America in 1780 my services were less brilliant and less useful than I would have desired. My passage to America on *l'Ariel*, frigate of the king,

---

[74] See letters concerning Stack and MacCarthy in the documentary evidence section of this memoir. The Society of the Cincinnati was a fraternal order of revolutionary war officers, founded in 1783. On special occasions members wore the society emblem, but it was not an official decoration of the American government.

was of some utility, however, in delivering important dispatches to the minister plenipotentiary to Congress, as well as for the fleet and army of France. And the sword with which His Majesty honored me was not degraded in the fight between l'*Ariel* and the *Triumph*.

May I be permitted to say that, if I had not been entrusted with the construction and preservation of the *America*, if I had not sacrificed 18 months of my time and procured at my own expense the means of guarding it from the enemy during that time, this warship would never have appeared on the roster of the royal navy of France.[75]

As Jamaica was better known by me than by any other officer assigned to the projected expedition against that island, I presumed that I could render some services in that campaign; at least I showed my good intentions by embarking with the marquis de Vaudreuil.

Personal gain was never the reason for my public actions; I had more noble motives. And far from making my fortune from the Revolution that took place in America, I consecrated to this great cause the 10 best years of my life, without interruption, as well as my rest and a part of my fortune and my blood.

During the entire period of my connection with the court of Versailles, I served without salary, as a volunteer; the losses I suffered on the *Bonhomme Richard* when it sank and in the mutiny of the *Alliance* at Lorient added to my extraordinary expenses over a very long period of time amounted to at least 200,000 livres for which I never requested indemnity.

On December 20, 1783, the king was kind enough to instruct the maréchal de Castries to inform me "*that His Majesty would be very pleased to further my interests.*" This is all the more flattering to me since it was in relation to the letter that His Majesty ordered M. de Sartine, then minister of marine, to write to Congress in my favor on May 30, 1780, in which it is said that "the king would like to add his commendation and favors to the public acclaim. He has expressly charged me to inform you how satisfied he is with the services of the commodore; convinced that Congress will render him the same justice, etc. . . ."

---

[75] When surveyed at Brest in 1786 the ship was found to be riddled with dry rot and the Ministry of Marine condemned Jones' pride and joy. Morison, *Jones*, p. 329.

Among several proofs of the generosity of His Majesty in regard to the republic then being born in America, that of putting a squadron under the flag of Congress contributed greatly to assure His Majesty of the lasting gratitude of the United States. And perhaps the time will arrive sooner than one would think when I will have an occasion to merit the flattering compliments with which M. de Sartine honored me, when he, as minister of marine, sent me the sword of His Majesty on June 28, 1780, with these words: "His Majesty has had a sword of gold made for you that will be presented to you soon; and he has the greatest confidence in the use you will make of it for his glory and that of the United States."

EPILOGUE

Having received from the court of France the amount representing prize shares belonging to the citizens of the United States, according to the settlement reported in my journal, I returned to America on a French packet boat to terminate the transaction. It may be observed that the government of the United States is above the kind of pride *that prevents a reexamination of the past.* In America, the most flattering testimonial one can give a military man is *to strike a gold medal in his honor and present it to him.* These attestations of public esteem are very rare and have only been accorded to six officers. First, to General Washington, commander in chief, for taking Boston. Second, to General Gates for the capture of General Burgoyne's army. Third, to General Wayne, for the capture of Stony-Point, where the garrison was much stronger than the attackers. Fourth, to General Morgan for having fought and destroyed a detachment of 1,100 officers and soldiers, among the best troops of England, with only 900 militiamen. Fifth, to General Greene, for winning a decisive victory over the enemy at Eutaw Springs. But all of these medals, although certainly well deserved, were awarded in moments of enthusiasm. I had the unique satisfaction to receive the same honor, by a *unanimous* vote of the United States, assembled in Congress on October 16, 1787, in memory of the services I had rendered eight years before.

This section, which also appears in the king's copy at the Archives nationales (Marine MM 851), was probably written almost two years after the major portion of the memoir had been completed. Jones probably did not present a copy of it to the king until early in 1788, on his return from the United States.

DOCUMENTARY EVIDENCE

Copy of a letter from M. de Sartine to Mr. Huntington, President of the Congress of the United States of America

Versailles, May 30, 1780

Commodore Paul Jones, after having shown Europe, and particularly the enemies of France and the United States, definite proof of his valor and skill, is returning to America and should render an account of the success of his military operations to Congress. I know, Sir, that he will be preceded by the reputation he has so justly acquired, and that the account of his campaigns alone will suffice to prove to his countrymen that his skill is equal to his courage; but the king would like to add his commendation and *favors* to the public acclaim. He has expressly charged me to inform you how satisfied he is with the services of the commodore; convinced that Congress will render him the same justice, he has hastened to give proof of this by presenting him a sword, which could not be put in better hands, as a gift and offers Congress to decorate this brave officer with the Croix du mérite militaire. His Majesty thought that this particular distinction, by holding forth the same honor to the two nations, which are united by common interests, could be regarded as one more tie that connects them and could sustain the emulation so necessary to the common cause. If after having approved the conduct of the commodore, Congress decides to send him on some new expedition to Europe, His Majesty would see him again with pleasure and presumes that Congress would oppose nothing that was felt to be necessary to ensure the success of his enterprises. My personal esteem for him leads me to recommend him particularly to you, sir, and I dare flatter myself that in the reception he receives from Congress and from you, he will recognize the effect of the sentiments with which he has inspired me.

I have the honor to be &c.

Signed De Sartine

[Translation]

———————————◆•◆———————————

Versailles, June 28, 1780

The king, sir, has already testified to his approbation for the zeal and valor you have displayed in Europe in support of the common cause with the United States of America; and His Majesty, at the same time, has informed you of the marks of distinction he is disposed to grant you. Convinced that the United States will give their consent that you should receive the Croix de l'Institution du Mérite Militaire, I am sending the award designated for you to M. de la Luzerne in the accompanying dispatch packet. You will be pleased to deliver this packet to him and he will have you received as a chevalier of that institution according to the orders of His Majesty. But, so that in any case you should have testimony of the satisfaction and generosity of the king, His Majesty had a gold sword made for you which will be delivered without delay, and he has the greatest confidence that you will use it for his glory and that of the United States.

I have the honor to be &c.

Signed De Sartine

Paul Jones, Commodore of the United States Navy at Lorient

[Translation]

———————————◆•◆———————————

Versailles, August 15, 1780

Sir, I have received with pleasure and read with attention the letter you wrote me from Lorient on the second of this month; I have seen in it your continuing zeal for the common cause. I have studied the plan[1] that was attached to your letter

---

[1] This is Jones' plan to recruit sailors and officers in America to serve on a fleet of French ships which he would command.

and communicated it to M. de Sartine, and we do not doubt the good effect that would result if its execution were to be entrusted to you; but at this moment it could not be said what number of frigates might be employed. They are all presently manned and rigged at the king's expense, and the plan for the next campaign is not sufficiently determined to say positively how many frigates would be available for your goal. But, if you have the agreement of Congress, this need not prevent the execution of the first part of your plan to come here as you proposed with the *Alliance* and other ships you may have, and with an American crew sufficient to man the frigates that may join you here. Between now and then I will try to secure some for you or to replace them by privateers. This is all I can inform you of for the present. The conduct you have displayed and the zeal you have shown for the service must assure you of the readiness with which I will always aid any enterprises in which you share. You can be sure, Sir, of the desire that I have of rendering you any service and convincing you of the sentiments with which I am &c.

Signed Maurepas

Commodore Paul Jones at Lorient

[Translation]

◆ ◆ ◆

IN CONGRESS

Tuesday, February 27, 1781

On report of a Committee, consisting of Mr. Sharpe, Mr. McDougall, and Mr. Sullivan, to whom was referred a letter of 30th May from Monsieur de Sartine.

Resolved, That Congress entertain a high sense of the distinguished bravery and military conduct of John Paul-Jones, Esquire, Captain in the navy of the United-States; and particularly in his victory over the British ship of War Serapis, on the coast of England, which was attended with circumstances so brilliant, as to excite general applause and admiration.

That the minister plenipotentiary of these United States, at the court of Versailles, communicate to his most Christian Majesty the high satisfaction Congress have received from the information of Monsieur de Sartine, that the conduct and gallant behaviour of Captain John Paul-Jones have merited the attention and approbation of his most Christian Majesty, and that his Majesty's offer of adorning Captain Paul-Jones with the Cross of military Merit, is highly acceptable to Congress.

———————— ◆•◆ ————————

By the United-States in Congress assembled

Saturday, April 14, 1781

On the report of a committee, consisting of Mr. Varnum, M Houston, and Mr. Mathews, to whom was referred a motion of Mr. Varnum: The United States in Congress assembled having taken into consideration the report of the board of admiralty of the 28th March last, respecting the conduct of John Paul-Jones, Esquire captain in the navy do.

Resolve, That the thanks of the United States in Congress assembled, be given to Captain John Paul-Jones, for the zeal, prudence, and intrepidity with which he hath supported the honour of the American flag, for his bold and successful enter-prizes to redeem from captivity the citizens of these States who had fallen under the power of the enemy; and in general for the good conduct and eminent services by which he has added lustre to his character and to the American arms:

That the thanks of the United-States in Congress assem-bled, be also given to the officers and men who have faithfully served under him from time to time, for their steady affection to the cause of their country, and the bravery and perseverance they have manifested therein.

———————— ◆•◆ ————————

Headquarters New-Windsor 15th mai 1781

Sir

My partial acquaintance with Either our Naval and Commercial Affairs, Makes it altogether impossible for me to

80

account for the unfortunate delay of those articles of military stores and Cloathing which have been so long provided in France.

Had I have had any particular reasons to have suspected you of being accessary to that delay, which I assure you has not been the case, my suspicions would have been removed by the very full and satisfactory answers which you have, to the best of my judgment, made to the questions proposed to you by the Board of admiralty and upon which that Board have in their report to Congress testified the high sense Which They entertain of your Merit and Services.

Whether our Naval affairs have in general been well or ill conducted would be presumptuous in me to determine. Instances of bravery and good conduct in several of our officiers have not however been Wanting: Delicacy forbids me to mention that Particular one which has attracted the admiration of all the World, and which has influenced the Most illustrious Monarch to confer a mark of his favor, which can only be obtained by a long and honourable Service, or by the Performance of some Brilliant action.

That you may long enjoy the Reputation you have so justly acquired is the sincere wish of
Sir, Your Most obedient and very humble Servant
Signed George Washington
The Chevalier Paul-Jones Captain in the Navy of the United-States.

----◆•◆----

By the United-States in Congress assembled
Saturday, June 23, 1781
A committee, consisting of Mr. Clymer, Mr. Sullivan, Mr. Mathews, to whom were referred two letters of 22d. from Mr. R. Morris delivered in a report; Whereupon,

Resolved That Robert Morris Esquire, be and he is hereby, authorized and directed to take measures for the spedily launching and equipping for sea the ship *America* now on the stocks at Portsmouth in New-Hampshire.

----◆•◆----

By the United-States in Congress assembled
Friday June 26, 1781
Congress proceeded to the appointment of a Captain to Command the ship *America;* and the ballots being taken.
John Paul-Jones, Esquire, was *unanimously* elected.

———————◆•◆———————

Alliance, off Boston decr. 22d, 1781
I have been honored with your polite favor, my dear Paul-Jones; but before it reached me I already was on board the Alliance, and every Minute expecting to put to sea. It would have afforded me great satisfaction to pay my respects to the inhabitants of Portsmouth, and the State in which you are for the present. As to the pleasure to take you by the hand, My dear Paul-Jones, you Know my affectionate sentiments, and my very great regard for you, so that I Need not add any thing on theat subject.

Accept of my best thanks for the Kind expressions in your letter. His Lordship's (Lord Cornwalis) downfall is a great event, and the greater as it was equaly and amicably shared by the two allied Nations. Your coming to the Army I had the honor to command would have been considered as a very flattering compliment to me who loves you and Knows your worth. I am impatient to hear you are ready to sail, and I am of opinion we ought to unite under you every continental ship we can Muster, with such a body of well appointed Marines (Troupes de Mer) as might cut a good figure ashore and then give you plenty of provision and *Carte Blanche.*

I am sorry I cannot see you: I also had many things to tell you. Write me by good opportunities, but not often in Cyphers unless the Matter is very important. On my arrival in France, I will be able to let you Know about the one you gave me, but am almost certain I have got it.

Your friends will be happy to hear from you: and I, my dear Sir, Need to tell you that your letters will be gratifully acknowledged by &c.
Signed La Fayette
To John Paul-Jones Esqr. Chevalier of Royal order of Military Merit, Commander of the Ship-of-the-Line America, at Portsmouth in New-Hampshire.

By the United-States in Congress assembled
Monday, May 13, 1782

Ordered, That a letter be written to the commander in chief and to the commander in the Southern department, by the Secretary for foreign affairs informing them of the public annonciation of the birth of the Dauphin, that the same may be published in both armies with Such demonstrations of joy as their Commanders shall respectively direct.

That the Secretary for foreign affairs also inform the governos and presidents of the respective States, of the birth of an heir to the crown of France that the people of each state may partake in the joy which an event that so nearly affects the happiness of their great and generous ally cannot fail to excite.

Philadelphia, July 29, 1782

Sir,

I have received the letter that you honored me by writing the 24th of June last. The details of the celebration of the birth of the dauphin and the part that you have played will be sent to France, and your efforts to express your attachment for a country in which your actions have inspired the highest esteem will surely give pleasure there.

Be certain of the good wishes, sir, that I have for you and the unending attachment with which I have the honor to be,
Signed the chevalier de la Luzerne

Mr. Paul-Jones.

⟦Translation⟧

Hague augst. 12th, 1782

Dear Sir,

I had yesterday the pleasure of receiving your favor of the 10th of December last, and am much obliged to you for your care of the articles, which Mr. Moyland at my Desire sent to my family.

The Command of the *America* could not have been more judiciously bestowed, and it is with impatience that I wish her at sea, where she will do honor to her name. Nothing gives me so much surprise, or so much regret as the inattention of my Countrymen to their navy: it is to us a Bulwark, as essential, as it is to great Britain. It is less Costly than Armies, and more easily removed from one end of the United States to the other. Our Minister of finance used to be a great advocate for this Kind of deffence. I hope he has not altered his sentiments concerning it.

Everyday shews that the Batavians[2] have not wholly lost their antient Character. They were always timid and slow in adopting their Political Systems; but always firm and able in support of them, and always brave and active in War. They have hitherto been restrained by their Chiefs; but if the War continues, they will shew that they are possessed of the spirit of Liberty and that they have lost none of their great qualities.

Rodney's victory[3] has intoxicated Britain again to such a degree that I think there will be no peace for some time. Indeed if I could see a prospect of having half-a-dozen line-of-Battle-Ships under the American flag, commanded by Commodore Paul-Jones, engaged with an equal British force, I apprehend the event would be so glorious for the United-States, and lay so sure a fondation for their Prosperity that it would be a rich compensation for a continuance of the War.

However, it does not depend upon us to finish it. There is but one way and that Burgoyneizing *Carlton*[4] in New-York.

I should be happy to hear from you and remain, Sir

Your most obedient and humble Servant.

Signed John Adams

J. Paul-Jones Esquire Commander of the *America* at Portsmouth, New Hampshire.

———————— ◆ • ◆ ————————

[2] Batavians are inhabitants of the Lowlands, i.e., Dutchmen.
[3] Battle off Saints Passage, April 9–12, 1782. Admiral George B. Rodney defeated a French fleet and captured its admiral, the comte de Grasse.
[4] Adams apparently meant that Sir Guy Carleton and his army would have to be forced to surrender in New York, just as British Gen. John Burgoyne and his army had been captured at Saratoga in 1777.

By the United States in Congress Assembled

Tuesday September 3, 1782

On motion of Mr. Osgood, seconded by Mr. Williamson.

Whereas the Magnifique, a seventy four-gun-ship belonging to the fleet of his most Christian Majesty, Commanded by the marquis de Vaudreuil, has been lately lost by accident in the harbour of Boston, and Congress are desirous of testifying on this occasion of his Majesty, the Sense they entertain of his generous exertions in behalf of the United-States:

Resolved, That the agent of marine be and he is hereby instructed to present the *America* a Seventy-four-Gun-ship, in the name of the United-States, to the Chevalier de la Luzerne for the Service of his Most Christian Majesty.

Marine office 4th September 1782

Dear Sir,

The enclosed Resolution will shew you the destination of the ship *America*. Nothing could be more pleasing to me than this disposition, excepting so far as you are affected by it. I Know you so well as to be convinced that it must give you great Pain, and I Sincerely sympathize with you; But although you will undergo Much Concern at being deprived of this opportunity to reap Laurels on your favorite field, yet your Regard for France will in some measure alleviate it, and to this your good sense will naturally add the delays which must have happened in fitting this ship for sea. I Must intreat of you to continue your Inspection until she is launched, and to urge forward the Business. When that is done if you will come hither, I will explain to you the reason which led to this Measure, and my views for employing you in the Service of your Country. You will on your Route have an opportunity of conferring with the General, on the Plan You mentioned to me in One of your letters.

I pray you to believe me with the most Sincere Esteem and Respect

Your affectionate Friend &
obedient Servant
Signed Robert Morris

Chevalier Paul-Jones. Portsmouth

Marine Office 9th October 1782

Sir

    I have received your letter of the twenty-second of last Month. The sentiments contained in it will always reflect the highest honor upon your Character. They have made so strong an Impression upon My Mind that I immediately transmitted an Extract of your Letter to Congress. I doubt not but they will view it in the same manner which I have done.

    I am, Sir
        With very Sincere Esteem
        Your Most Obedient and humble Servant
        Signed Robert Morris
Chevalier Paul-Jones Portsmouth

By the United States in Congress assembled
        Wednesday, December 4, 1782
    Resolved, That the Agent of marine be, informed that Congress, having a high sense of the merit and services of captain John Paul-Jones, and being disposed to favour the Zeal manifested by him to acquire improvement in the line of his profession, do grant the permission Which he requests; and that the said Agent be instructed to recommend him accordingly, to the countenance of his Excellency the Marquis de Vaudreuil.

    Copy of a Letter from his Excellency the Marquis de Vaudreuil, Lieutenant Général of the Navy of France, Commandant of the Royal and Military order of St. Louis, Commanding the Squadron of his Most Christian Majesty in the West Indies; to his Excellency the Chevalier de la Luzerne, Minister Plenipotentiary of France in *America*.

Sir,

        Off the Cape, April 20, 1783
    The peace which has been so much desired, and which is going to make the happiness of America because it puts the seal

to her liberty, terminates all our projects. We shall sail in a week for France with the troops under the command of the baron de Viomenil; the other regiments will sail as soon as there are vessels ready to transport them.

Mr. Paul Jones, who had embarked with me, is returning to his dear country. I was very glad to have him: his well-deserved reputation had made me accept him with pleasure, not doubting but that we would have had some opportunities in which his talents might have shone forth. But peace, of which I cannot but be glad, puts an obstacle in the way; so we must part. Permit me, sir, to request of you the favor of recommending him to his superiors. The intimate acquaintance which I made with him since he has been on board *le Triomphant* makes me take a keen interest in him, and I shall be very much obliged to you if you are able to render him service.

Peace will not restore you to your country. On account of the great services which you render to France, it will be necessary for you to remain in America for a long time; but you have the consolation to be among a people who love and respect you: thus it is for you a second home, which you have acquired by your virtues and talents.

I am &c.

Signed the marquis de Vaudreuil

[Translation]

———————◆◆———————

Copy of a Letter from his Excellency the Marquis de Vaudreuil, . . . to his Excellency Robert Morris Esqr. Minister of Finance of the United-States of America.

Off the Cape, April 21, 1783

Sir,

The well-deserved reputation that Mr. Paul-Jones had when he embarked on the squadron I command made me desirous of finding some occasion where his talents could flourish.

The peace, which is so welcome to the nation, places an insurmountable obstacle there, and forces his departure to his dear fatherland. Permit me, sir, to beg you to render him any service in your power. The particular acquaintance that I made with him since he was on board *le Triomphant* gives me a keen interest in this brave and honest man.

I know, sir, that you are also interested in him, and thus I do not need to press you to render service to him.

I have the honor to be &c.

Signed, the marquis de Vaudreuil

[Translation]

————◆◆◆————

Copy of a Letter Written by his Excellency the Baron de Viomenil, grand-Croix of the Royal and Military order of St. Louis, Maréchal de Camp, Commanding in Chief the Army of France embarked on board the squadron of his Most Christian Majesty under the orders of the Marquis de Vaudreuil (Intended for the expédition against Jamaica), to his excellency the Chevalier de la Luzerne Minister plenipotentiary of France in America.

Off the Cap St. Domingue, April 21, 1783

Mr. Paul-Jones, who will have the honor of delivering this letter, sir, has for five months shown us a sagacity and modesty which adds infinitely to the reputation he has acquired by his actions and his courage. It seemed to me, moreover, that he maintained as much gratitude and attachment for France as patriotism and devotion for the cause of America. It is for all these reasons, sir, that I take the liberty of recommending to you the interest of this officer in the service of the first President and the members of Congress. It is, moreover, with the greatest pleasure that I take this occasion to assure you of the fidelity and fond attachment with which I have the honor to be

Signed Viomenil

[Translation]

————◆◆◆————

To the Honorable John Paul-Jones Commodore in the Service of the United-States of America.

In Pursuance of a Resolution of Congress of the first of November 1783 a Copy wereof is hereunto annexed, I do hereby authorize and direct you to Sollicit as agent for payment and satisfaction to the officiers and crews, Citizens or subjects of the Said States, for all Prizes taken in Europe under your Command and to which they are any wise intitled, and in whose hands soever the Prize-money may be detained.

Given at Passy this seventeenth of December 1783.

Signed B. Franklin

Minister Plenipotentiary from the United-States of America at the Court of France.

————◆◆◆————

Passy, March 25, 1784

Sir,

I return herewith the Papers you communicated to me yesterday. I perceive by the extract from M. de Sartine's Letter, that it was his intention all the charges which had accru'd upon the *Serapis* and *Countess of Scarborough* should be deducted from the Prize-money payable to the Captors, *particularly the expence of victualing the seamen & Prisonners;* and that the liquidation of those charges should be referr'd to me. This liquidation however never was referr'd to me; and if it had, I should have been cautious of acting in it, having received no power from the captors, either French or Americans, authorizing me to decide upon any thing respecting their interests. And I certainly should not have agreed to charge the American Captors with any Part of the Expence of maintaining the 500 prisoners in Holland till they could be exchanged, when none of them were exchanged for Americans in England, as was your intention, and *as we both had been made to expect.*

With great Esteem, I have the honor to be

Sir

Your most obedient humble servant

Signed B. Franklin

Honorable Paul-Jones Esqr. Paris.

————◆◆◆————

On board the Frigate Ranger at Brest
May 8th. 1778

Madam

It cannot be too much lamented that, in the profession of arms, the officer of fine feeling and real sensibility should be under the necessity of winking at any action of persons under his Command which his heart cannot approve; but the reflection is doubly severe when he finds himself obliged, in appearance, to countenance such action by his authority.

This hard case was mine, When, on the 23d of april last, I landed on St. Mary's Isle (presqu' Isle in Scotland). Knowing Lord Selkirk's interest with his King, and esteeming, as I do, his private caracter, I wished to make him the happy instrument of alleviating the horrors of hopeless captivity when the brave are overpowered and made Prisonners of War. It was perhaps fortunate for you, Madam, that he was from home; for it was my intention to have taken him on board the Ranger, and to have detained him until, through his means, a general and fair exchange of prisonners, as well in Europe as in America, had been effected.

When I was informed by some Men whom I met at landing, that his Lordship was absent, I walked back to my boat, determined to leave the Island. By the way however, some officers who were with me, could not forbear expressing their discontent; observing "that, in America, No delicacy was Shewn by the English, who took away all sorts of Movable property, Setting fire not only to Towns, and to the Houses of the Rich without distinction, but not even sparing the wretched hamlets, and Milch-Cows of the poor and helpless at the approach of an inclement Winter."

That party had been with me as volunteers, the same morning at Whitehaven (in England)—some complaisance there-fore was their due. I had but a moment to think how I Might gratify them, and, at the same time, do your Ladyship the least injury.

I charged the two officers to permit none of the Seamen to enter the house, or to hurt any thing about it—to treat you, Madam, with the utmost respect—to accept the plate which was offered—and to come away without making a Search or demanding any thing else. I am induced to believe that I was punctually obeyed; since I am informed that the plate which

90

they brought away is far short of the quantity expressed in the inventory which accompanied it.

I have gratifyed my Men, and, When the Plate is sold, I shall become the purchaser, and will gratify my own feelings by restoring it to you, by such conveyance as you shall please to direct.

Had the Earl been on board the Ranger the following evening, he would have seen the awful pomp, and dreadful carnage, of a sea engagement; both, affording ample subject for the pencil, as well as Melancholy reflection for the contemplative Mind. Humanity starts back from such scenes of horror, and cannot but execrate the vile promoters of this detested war.

For *they* 'twas *they* unsheath'd the ruthless blade,
And, Heaven shall ask the havock it has made.

The British ship of war Drake, mounting 20 guns, with more than her full complement of officers and men, besides a Number of Volunteers, came out from Carrick-fergus (in Ireland) in order to attack and take the American continental ship of war Ranger of 18 Guns, and short of her complement of officers & men. The ships met, (between Scotland and Ireland) & the advantage was disputed with great fortitude on each side for an hour five Minutes, when the Gallant Commander of the Drake fell, and victory declared in favor of the Ranger. His amiable Lieutenant lay Mortally Wounded, besides Forty of the inferior officers & Crew Kill'd and wounded: a Melancholy demonstration of the uncertainty of human prospects and of the Sad reverse of Fortune which an hour can produce. I buried them in a spacious grave (the ocean) with the honors due the memory of the brave.

Though I have drawn my sword in the present generous struggle for the Rights of Men, yet I am not in arms *merely* as an American; Nor am I in pursuit of Riches. My fortune is liberal enough, having no wife nor family, and having lived long enough to Know that Riches cannot ensure happiness.

I profess myself a Citizen of the World, totally unfettered by the little mean distinctions of climate or of country; which diminish the benevolence of the heart, and set bounds to Philanthropy. Before this War began I had, as an early time of life withdrawn from the sea-service, in favor of calm contemplation and poetic ease. I have sacrificed not only my favorite scheme of life, but *the softer affections of my heart*, and my prospects of domestic happiness: and I am ready to sacrifice my life also with chearfulness, if that forfeiture could restore peace and good will among mankind.

As the humain feelings of your gentle bosom cannot but be congenial with Mine, let me intreat you, Madam, to use your soft persuasive arts with your husband to endeavour to stop this cruel and destructive war in which Britain Never can succeed. Heaven can never countenance the barbarous and unmanly practices of the Britons in America; which savages would blush at, and which, if not discontinued, will soon be retaliated, in Britain, by a justly enraged people. Should you fail in this (for I am persuaded you will attempt it, and who can resist the power of such an advocate!) your endeavours to effect a general exchange of prisoners will be an act of humanity, which will afford you golden-feelings on a death-bed.

I hope this cruel contest will soon be closed; but, should it continue, I wage No War with the Fair. I acknowledge their power and bend before it with profound submission! Let not therefore the amiable countess of Selkirk regard me as an Enemy. I am ambitious of her esteem and friendship, and would do anything consistent with my duty, to merit it. The honor of a line from your hand, in answer to this, will lay me under a very singular obligation; and if I can render you any acceptable service, in France or elsewhere, I hope you see into my Character so far as to command me, without the least grain of reserve. I wish to Know exactly the behaviour of my people; as I determine to punish them, if they have exceeded their liberty. I have the honor to be with Much Esteem and profound Respect,

Madam

> Your Ladyship's Most obedient
> and most humble Servant
> (Signed) Paul-Jones

To the right honorable the Countess of Selkirk, in Scotland.

On board the Serapis at the Texel
Octr. 19, 1779

My Lord

Human nature, and America, are under very Singuler obligation to you, for your Patriotism and friendship; and I feel every grateful sentiment for your generous and polite letter.

Agreeable to your Request, I have the honor to inclose a copy of my letter to his Excellency Dr. Franklin; containing a particular account of my late expedition on the coast of Britain and Ireland; by which you will see, that I have already been praised more than I have deserved: But I must, at the same time, beg leave to observe that, by the other Papers which I take the liberty to enclose (particularly the Copy of my letter to the Countess of Selkirk, dated the day of my arrival at Brest from the Irish-sea), I hope you will be convinced that, in the British Prints, I have been censured unjustly. I was indeed born in Britain, but I do not inherit the degenerate spirit of that fallen Nation, which I at once lament and dispise. It is far beneath me to reply to their hireling invectives: they are strangers to the inward approbation, that greatly animates and rewards the Man, who draws his sword only in support of the dignity of Freedom.

America has been the Country of my fond election, from the age of thirteen, when I first saw it. I had the honor to hoist, with my hands, the flag of Freedom, the first time it was displayed on the River Delaware; and I have attended it, with veneration, ever since on the ocean. I see it respected, even here, in spite of the pitiful Sir Joseph (Sir Joseph York); and I ardently wish, and hope very soon, to exchange a salute with the flag of this Republic. Let but the two Republicks join hands, and they will give Peace to the World.

Highly ambitious to render myself worthy of your friend- ship, I have the honor to be, My Lord, your very obliged, and most humble Servant &c.

(Signed)   Paul-Jones

To the Baron Vander Capellen &c. at Amsterdam

———◆•◆———

On board the Alliance at the Texel
Novr. 29th 1779

My Lord

Since I had the honor to receive your second esteemed Letter, I have, unexpectedly, had occasion to revisit Amsterdam, and, having changed ships since my return to the Texel, I have, by some accident or neglect, lost or mislaid your letter. I remember, however, the questions it contained, vizt 1st. Whether I ever had any obligation to Lord Selkirk? 2dly. Whether he accepted my offer? and 3dly. Whether I have a french Commission? I answer, I never had any obligation to Lord Selkirk except for his good opinion; nor does he Know me or mine except by Character. Lord Selkirk wrote me in answer to my letter to the Countess; but the Ministry detained it in the general Post-office in London for a long time, and then returned it to the author; who afterwards wrote to a friend of his (Mr. Alexander) an acquaintance of Dr. Franklin's, then at Paris, giving him an account of the fate of his Letter to me, and desiring him to acquaint his Excellency and myself that, "if the Plate was Restored by Congress, or by any Public Body, he would accept it, but that he could not think of accepting it from my Private generosity."

The Plate has, however, been bought, agreable to my letter to the Countess, and now lays in France at her disposal. As to the 3d. article, I never bore, nor acted under, any other Commission than What I have received from the Congress of the United-States of America.

I am much obliged to you, Mylord, for the honor you do me by Proposing to Publish the Papers I sent you in my last; but it is an honor which I must decline, because I cannot Publish my letter to that Lady Without asking and obtaining the Lady's consent, and because I have a very modest opinion of my writings, being conscious that they are not of sufficient value to claim the notice of the Public:—I assure you, My Lord, it has given me much concern to see an extract of my rough journal in Print, and that too under the disadvantage of a translation: That mistaken kindness of a friend will make me cautious how I communicate my Papers.

I have the honor to be, My Lord, With great esteem and Respect &c.　　　　　　　　　　　(Signed)　Paul-Jones
To the Barren Vander Capellen &c. Amsterdam.

My Lord,

I have just received a Letter from Mr. Nesbitt, dated at Lorient the 4th instant, mentioning a letter to him from your son Lord Dare [Daer]; on the subject of the Plate, that was taken from your House by some of my People when I commanded the Ranger, and has been for a long time past in Mr. Nesbitt's care.

A short time before I left France to return to America, M. W. Alexander wrote me from Paris to Lorient, that he had, at my request, seen and conversed with your Lordship in England respecting the Plate. He said you had agreed that I should restore it, and that it might be forwarded to the care of your sister-in-Law the Countess of Morton in London. In consequence I now send orders to M. Nesbitt, to forward the Plate immedeately to her care.

When I received M. Alexander's letter, there was no cartel or other vessel at Lorient, that I could trust with a charge of so delicate a nature as your Plate; and I had great reason to expect I should have returned to France, within six months after I embarked for America. But circumstances, in America, prevented my returning to Europe during the War, though I had constant expectation of it.

The long delay that has happened to the restoration of your Plate has given me much concern, and I now feel a proportionate Pleasure in fulfilling what was my first intention. My motive for Landing at your Estate in Scotland was to take *you*, as an *Hostage*, for the lives and liberty of a number of the Citizens of America, who had been taken in war on the Ocean and commited to British Prisons under an Act of Parlement as "*Traitors, Pyrates and Fellons.*" You observed to M. Alexander that my idea was a mistaken one; because you were not (as I had supposed) in favor with the British Ministry, who knew "*that you favored the cause of Liberty.*" On that account, I am glad that you were absent from your Estate when I landed there; as I bore no Personal enmity, but the Contrary towards you. I afterwards had the happiness to redeem my fellow-Citizens from Britain, by means far more glorious than through the medium of any single hostage.

95

As I have endeavoured to serve the cause of Liberty Through every stage of the American Revolution, and sacrificed to it my private ease, a part of my fortune, and some of my Blood, I could have no selfish motive in permitting my People to demand and Carry off your Plate. My sole inducement was to turn their attention and stop their rage from breaking out, and retalliating on your house and Effects the *too wanton* Burnings and desolation, that had been Committeed against their relations and fellow-Citizens in America, by the British; of which, I assure you, you would have felt the severe consequence, had I not fallen on an expedient to prevent it, and hurried my People away before they had time for further reflection.

As you were so obliging as to say to Mr. Alexander, *"that my People beheaved with great decency at your House."* I ask the favor of you to annonce that circumstance to the Public. I am, My Lord, wishing you always perfect freedom and Happiness.

Your Lordship's most obedient
and most humble servant
(Signed)   Paul Jones

To the right honorable, the Earl of Selkirk in Scotland.

———◆•◆———

Paris, September 24, 1784

The comte de Vergennes, Sir, has delivered to me the letter you had written him, to request his permission to transport by land from Lorient to Calais Lady Selkirk's plate, which you had permitted to be taken by your crew during the last war, and which you afterward purchased to return to her ladyship.

That action, sir, is worthy of the reputation which you acquired by your conduct and proves that true valor perfectly agrees with humanity and generosity.

It gives me great pleasure to concur in the execution of this honorable proceeding.

I have, therefore, given orders to the Farmers General to permit the transportation of the plate from Lorient to Calais, free of duty, and you may write to your correspondent at

Lorient to deliver it to the director of the posts, who will take upon himself the care of having it transported to Calais and fulfill all the necessary formalities.

I have the honor to be, &c.

Signed De Calonne

Mr. Paul Jones, Naval Captain at Paris

[Translation]

--------◆•◆--------

Paris Novr. 8th 1784

Madam,

Since the moment when I found myself under the necessity to permit my Men to demand and carry off your Family-Plate, it has been my constant intention to restore it to you; and I wrote you to that effect from Brest, the moment I had arrived there from my expedition in the Irish-sea.

By the letter I had the honor to write your husband the 12th of feby. last, which will accompany this, I have explained the difficulties that prevented the plate from being restored until that time. I had expectation, all the last summer that opportunities would have offered to send it by sea, from Lorient to London; but being disappointed, I applied to Government for leave to transport it through this Kingdom by land; and the Duke of Dorset has been so obliging as to write to the Custom-house at Dover, requesting them to let it pass to London, without being opened. It is now arrived here, and will be forwarded immediately to your Sister in London; under the Lead that has been affixed to the case that contains it by the farmers general at Lorient, and the Seal of the Duke of Dorset, that has been affixed to it here. The charges to London are paid; and I have directed it to be delivered at the house of your Sister.

I could have wished to have ended this delicate Business, by delivering the plate to you at St. Mary's Isle in Scotland; but I conform to the arrangement made between your husband and Mr. Alexander, because I have no person in London whom I can charge with the transportation of the plate from thence. Enclosed is the inventory that I have just received from Mr. Nesbitt from Lorient; which I presume you will find to corre-

97

spond with the one he sent last year to Lord Dare, and with the articles which you put into the hands of my Men.

I am, Madam, with Sentiments, of the highest respect.
Your Ladyship's most obedient
and most humble Servant
(Signed)   Paul-Jones
The Right honorable the Countess Selkirk in Scotland.

———————◆◆◆———————

London the 4th of august 1785
Sir,

I received the letter you wrote to me at the time you sent off my Plate, in order for Restoring it: had I known where to direct a letter to you, at the time it arrived in Scotland, I would have then wrote to you: but not Knowing it, nor finding that any of my acquaintances at Edinburgh Knew it, I was obliged to delay writing 'till I came here; when by means of a Gentlemen connected with America, I was told Mr. Le Grand was your Banker at Paris and would take Proper care of a Letter for you, therefore I inclose this to him.

Notwithstanding all the Precautions you took for the easy and uninterrupted conveyance of the Plate, yet it met with Considerable delays; first at Calais, next at Dover, then at London: however it at last arrived at Dumfries; and I dare say quite safe; though as yet I have not seen it, being then at Edinburgh.

I intended to have put an article in the News-Papers about your having returned it; but before I was informed of its being arrived, some of your friends, I suppose, had Put it in the Dumfries News-Paper; whence it was immediately copied into the Edinburgh Papers and thence into the London ones.

Since that time I have mentioned it to many people of fashion; and on all occasions Sir, Both now and formerly I have done you the justice to tell, that you made an offer of returning the Plate very soon after your return to Brest: and although you yourself was not at my house, but remaing at the shore with your Boat, that yet you had your officers and men in such extraordinairy good discipline, that you having given them the strictest orders to behave well, to do no injury

98

of any kind, to make no search, but only to bring off what Plate
was given them; that in reality they did exactly as ordered:
and that not one Man offerd to stir from his Post on the outside of the house, nor enterd the doors, nor said an uncivil
word: that the two officers staid not a quarter of an hour in
the parlour and Butler's pantry, while the Butler got the plate
together; behaved Politely, and asked for nothing but the Plate
and instantly marched their men off in regular order; and that
both officers and men behaved in all Respects so well, that it
would have done credit to the best disciplin'd Troops whatever.

Some of the English News-Papers, at that time, having
put in confused accounts of your expedition to White-haven
and Scotland, I ordered a proper one of what happend in Scotland to be put in the London News-Papers, by a Gentleman who
was then at my house; by which the good conduct and civil
behaviour of your officers and men was done justice to and attributed to your orders, and the good discipline you maintaind
over your people.

I am, Sir your most humble Servant

Signed   Selkirk
Monsieur Le Chevalier Paul-Jones at Paris.

--- ◆◆◆ ---

Paris, November 29, 1779
Having received, sir, the order of the court for the em-
barkment of my regiment's Second Battalion which is going to
fight in the Antilles, I find, you will see, that it is impossible
for you to remain on board ship with Commodore Paul Jones
because this would make it necessary for one of your comrades
to serve in your place. I do not know where to find you to give
you the present order to rejoin your company at Brest with all
possible speed, but I hope the duc de la Vauguyon, ambassador
of the king at The Hague, will be able to contact you. I will be
delighted on your arrival here to convey to you the thanks of
the king for your conduct in the brilliant fight of the American
commodore.

(Signed)   the comte de Walsh Serrant
Mr. Stack, officer in the Régiment de Walsh

[Translation]

Versailles, December 12, 1779

Upon the account that I rendered to the king, sir, of the conduct that you followed with Commodore Paul Jones in the fight against an English frigate of superior force that he mastered, His Majesty wishes to signify his satisfaction by granting you a commission as a brevet captain, while maintaining your lieutenancy, and an extraordinary reward of 400 livres.[5] I am pleased to give this to you and am &ca.

Signed   the prince de Montbarey

Mr. Stack (Edward), First Lieutenant in the Régiment de Walsh.

[Translation]

Versailles, February 27, 1785

Upon the account that I have delivered to the king, sir, of your services, and particularly the distinguished conduct that you followed on board the frigate the *Bonhomme Richard*, His Majesty wishes to signify his satisfaction by granting you a pension of 400 livres. I am pleased to present this to you and am etc.

Signed, the maréchal de Ségur

Mr. Stack, First Lieutenant, with the rank of captain in the Régiment de Walsh, Infantry.

[Translation]

Paris April 13, 1785

Edward Stack sub-Lieutenant in the Régiment of Walsh, in the service of his most Christian Majesty, had leave from

---

[5] Records of Stack's indicate that he was promoted and did receive a 400-livre award from the king because Jones certified that the victory over the *Serapis* was due in part to Stack's valor. See Stack's service records and recommendations in Bibliothèque du service historique de l'armée, Corps des troupes, Series Xb, Infanterie de Walsh–Serrant, fols. 142, 144–146.

the court of Versailles in the beginning of the year 1779 to serve on board the Squadron which his Majesty then put under my Command: As I had made it a condition with the Minister of Marine that the Squadron should carry the Flag of America, because I could not, (as an American officer,) accept the Commission of Captain in the Royal Navy of France, all the officers of the Squadron received from me (with the consent and approbation of Mr. Franklin) Brevets, that had been signed and sent Blank to Europe, by M. Hancock, as President of Congress. The Commission of Mr. Stack was that of Lieutenant of Marin-Troops, in the Navy of the United-States.

He served in that quality on board the Bon-homme Richard, and was in the engagement between that ship and the Serapis, on the coast of England, the 23d. day of September 1779.

At the Texel, in the month of November following, he received orders from France to join his Régiment, then ordered to embark for the West Indies; and on producing, at Versailles the Certificate I gave him at the Texel, his Majesty promoted him immediately to the Rank of Captain, with a Pecuniary gratification for the loss he sustained when the Bon-homme Richard sank, after the Battle.

But there can be no Clearer proof of the high sense his Majesty entertains of the merit of that Battle, than his having confered on Captain Stack, *on that account*, the Pension of four hundred livres a year the 27th. of February last.

Captain Stack has applied to me, and wishes to become a member of the Society of Cincinnatus. There is no doubt in my mind, but that he has merited that distinction. I am of opinion that the order he received at the Texel, ought to be considered as operating his derangement, and Plaecing in a similar predicament with the officers of the American Army, who were reformed by particular Acts of Congress, and who are notwithstanding entitled to become members of the Cincinnati.

If M. Stack, therefore, can obtain a similar opinion from their Excellency's Count D'Estaing, and Count de Rochambeau, and from the Marquis de la Fayette, the Marquis de Saint-Simon, and Colonel Humphrys, in writing, at the foot hereof, I have no doubt but that he will be considered in America as a member of the Society; when he has paid a month's pay into

the hands of Colonel Humphrys for the Charitable Fund of
the Society.

Signed   Paul-Jones

[Note: Letters of David Humphreys, the comte d'Estaing, the marquis de St. Simon, and the
marquis de Lafayette sustaining Jones' opinion of Stack are appended in the original. They are
not included here because the standard form of recommendation that is used does not contribute
anything to understanding either Jones or his activities.]

◆•◆

I, the undersigned, certify that after the capture of the English
vessel the *Serapis* by the *Bonhomme Richard,* and after it had
been decided to abandon this latter vessel because it was unable to float, the efforts on the part of Commodore Paul Jones
to transport the wounded and the impossibility of keeping that
boat afloat any longer prevented Mr. Paul Jones from saving
his personal effects, which sank along with those of the entire
crew.

Paris, April 17, 1785
Signed, MacCarthy[6]
Captain, Régiment de Walsh

[Translation]

[Note: An identical letter dated April 19, 1785, and signed by Edward Stack follows in the
original.][7]

◆•◆

Marine office Philadelphia Nov. 29th, 1782

Sir
    I do myself the honor to enclose to your Excellency the
Copy of a Letter received this morning from the Chevalier
Paul-Jones. The present state of our affairs does not permit me
to employ that valuable officer, and I confess that it is with no

---

[6] Eugene MacCarthy received a brevet commission as captain and a 400-livre gratification
for his service with Jones. See MacCarthy's records and recommendations, Bibliothèque du
service historique de l'armée, Corps des troupes, Series Xb, Infanterie de Walsh–Serrant,
fols. 164–66.
   [7] The king's copy of the memoir ends here with a note that the need to return to America
precludes further work.

small degree of concern that I consider the little probability of rendering his Talents useful to that Country, which he has already so faithfully served, and with so great disinterestdness. His present Desire* consists with all his former conduct, and it will, I dare say, be a very pleasing reflection to congress, that he is about to pursue a knowledge of his profession, so as to become still more useful if ever he should be again call'd to the Command of a Squadron or Fleet. I should do Injustice to my own feelings, as well as to my Country, If I did not most warmly recommend this Gentleman to the Notice of Congress, *whose favor he has certainly merited by the most Signal services and sacrifices.*

I have the honor to be &c.

(Signed)   R. Morris

his Excellency the President of Congress.

* To be sent with the Marquis de Vaudreuil, to join Count d'Estaing on his projected Expedition from Cadix, against Jamaica &c.

———————◆◆◆———————

Marine office Philadelphia 30th Sept. 1784

Sir

I am [writing] to acknowledge the receipt of your several favors of the 26th. of Decr., 13th. April and 18th. June last. I have to reproach myself, for not making an early reply to the first; but I was so much harrassed when I received it that I could not find an opportunity. Afterwards I lived in the daily expectation of making my personal acknowledgements; but since your stay in Europe has been delayed beyond either your expectation or mine, I now take the last opportunity which I shall ever have of expressing my sentiments *Officially* upon the *Zeal Activity Fortitude* and *Intelligence*, which you have exhibited on so many occasions in the service of the United States. Accept I pray you sir, this last feeble Testimony which I can give, and which, however unequal to your deserts, is at least expressive of that Respect and sincere Esteem with which I have the honor to be &c.

(Signed)   R. Morris

The Chevalier Paul-Jones—Paris

◆•◆

Paris, December 18, 1785

It is impossible, sir, not to take advantage of your kindness; do not lend me your journal again, because I must warn you that I shall read it over and over, and always with renewed pleasure. It is one of the things which one absolutely wants to know by heart. This lesson of military and naval heroism has, by your conduct to Lord and Lady Selkirk, also become one of generosity.

I am far from regretting the homage I have been obliged to render to the engagement between the *Bonhomme Richard* and the *Serapis*; and although I did not imagine, while writing it,[8] that it might be of any other use than that of procuring an admission into the Society of the Cincinnati, I cannot but be flattered that you have thought it proper to insert it among the pieces which are annexed to your journal.

I have the honor to be with the most perfect attachment,

(Signed)   Estaing

Mr. Paul Jones, Commodore of the United States at Paris

[Translation]

◆•◆

Paris, February 27, 1786

I have received, sir, with much gratitude the mark of confidence which you have given me, and I have read with great eagerness and pleasure that interesting account.

My first impulse was to desire you to have it published. But after having read it, I see that you have not written it with a view to publication, because there are things in it which are written only for the king, for whom alone the work is intended. However, actions as memorable as yours ought to be made known to the world by an authentic journal published in your own name.

I earnestly entreat you to work on it as soon as your affairs will allow you; and in the meantime, *I hope that the*

---

[8] Refers to his letter of recommendation for Edward Stack in which he described the engagement as "the most glorious naval battle not only of the last war, but of which the history of all nations has ever spoken. . . ."

king will read this work with the attention he owes to the relation of the services that have been rendered to him by a person so celebrated.

I beg you to be persuaded of the sincere attachment with which, I have the honor to be, &c.

(Signed)   Malesherbes

Mr. Paul Jones, Commodore in the service of the United States at Paris

[Translation]

———————◆•◆———————

By the United States Assembled in Congress
New York, October 16, 1787

It has been voted *unanimously* that a gold medal should be struck and presented to Commodore Paul Jones in commemoration of the valor and distinguished services of that officer during the time that he had command of a squadron of French and American ships of war off the coasts of Great Britain during the last war.

It has been voted that Mr. Jefferson, minister plenipotentiary of the United States to His Most Christian Majesty, should be instructed to have the same medal struck with the proper allegories, symbols, and inscriptions.

It has been voted that a letter should be written to His Most Christian Majesty to inform him that the United States has bestowed this medal on Commodore Paul Jones in consideration of the marks of approbation that His Majesty has deigned to give him as well as of his talents and merit. And as the most earnest desire of this officer is to acquire new knowledge in his profession, mention will be made in this letter of the pleasure Congress would have if His Majesty would grant him permission to embark on his fleets of evolution, Congress being convinced that nowhere else could he acquire that knowledge which may hereafter render him even more useful.

As a result, it has been ordered that the secretary of state for foreign affairs prepare, along these lines, a letter that will be signed by the President and confided to the Commodore Paul-Jones for him to present to His Majesty.

(Signed)   Charles Thomson
Secretary of the United States in Congress

[Translation]

Attestation of Mr. Van Berckel, grand-pensionnaire of Amsterdam, and of Mr. Dumas, United States agent in Holland.

Commodore Paul Jones, commander of a light squadron equipped at the expense of His Most Christian Majesty and under the flag and commission of the United States of America, sailed from France on August 14, 1779, during the time that the French and Spanish allied fleet of 66 ships of the line under the command of the comte d'Orvilliers appeared in the channel between France and England.[9] Because it was expected that a French army would land on the southern coast of England under cover of this fleet, the commodore, having carte blanche, believed his duty was to make a strong diversion to facilitate the enterprise. For this purpose, he alarmed and insulted the ports of the enemy from Cape Clear, along the western coast of Ireland, through the north of Scotland to Hull, and down the east side of England. During the course of this service, as difficult as it was important, he made several captures of armed ships and destroyed a number of the enemy's merchant vessels. The great desire of the commodore was to intercept the British fleet returning from the Baltic, and in this way to deprive the enemy of the means of equipping their warships. There is every reason to believe that he would have fully carried out this plan, if he had not been abandoned on the coast of Ireland by a considerable part of his force, and if his frigate, the *Bonhomme Richard*, had been in the least supported in its memorable battle with the *Serapis*, a two-decked ship, and against the *Countess of Scarborough*, a frigate. But after the commodore had been fighting the two ships alone for an hour at pistol range, while the rest of his forces remained out of the fight, despite the advantage of the wind, the *Alliance*, an American frigate, traitorously fired three broadsides into the *Bonhomme Richard*. During the entire affair, the *Alliance* was careful not to expose herself to a single blow; neither did she have a single man killed or wounded on board. The *Bonhomme Richard* was lashed to the *Serapis* for three hours, and after the battle, which lasted four hours, she sank, riddled by blows as no vessel had

---

[9] The abortive invasion and its diplomatic effects are discussed in Richard Morris, *The Peacemakers; the Great Powers and American Independence* (New York: Harper & Row, 1965), pp. 27–42.

ever been before. As the battle occurred within a league of Scarborough it was impossible, under the circumstances previously mentioned, to prevent the English convoy from entering this port, where they established themselves securely.

The commodore entered the Texel with the remainder of his squadron and his two last prizes on October 3, 1779. Half of the crews of the *Bonhomme Richard* and the *Serapis* having been killed or wounded, the commodore petitioned their High Mightinesses for permission to establish a hospital at Helder to be able to treat the wounded; but the local magistrates being opposed, their High Mightinesses allocated the fort of Texel for this purpose. And because the Commodore had permission to garrison that fort with a detachment of his soldiers, he assigned the charge of commander of the place to one of his officers, for as long as necessary.

The allied fleet having returned to Brest, the English, relieved of the fear of invasion that had menaced them, directed all their animosity against the commodore. The English ambassador at The Hague, by repeated memorials to the States General, never ceased demanding the restitution of the warship and frigate captured by the commodore and required besides that the Scottish *Pirate Paul-Jones* be delivered to the king, his master. This course not succeeding for the ambassador, he contacted all the magistrates and private citizens of Amsterdam and asked them to seize the commodore and deliver him over to him. But it was in vain: no one had the vileness or the effrontery to lend himself to his desires in this regard. The English detached several light squadrons to intercept the commodore. Two of the squadrons cruised continually within sight of the Texel and the Fly, while the others were stationed in such a manner as to convince them that it was impossible for him to escape them. The object of the court of France in having the commodore enter the Texel was so that he could escort to Brest a large fleet laden with material for the arsenal of that port. But his situation rendered this service impracticable, chiefly because the minister did not keep the plan a secret. The position of the commodore in the Texel had already attracted the attention of all Europe and would profoundly affect the policies of the belligerent powers. But this position became infinitely more critical when the prince of Orange removed Mr. Riemersma from his command of the Dutch fleet, which had 13

107

ships of war, and sent Vice Admiral Rhynst to succeed him and to expel the commodore from the Texel within sight of the British squadrons.

This led the court at Versailles to send the ambassador of France to The Hague a commission of His Most Christian Majesty for the commodore, which authorized him to hoist the French flag. But the commodore did not want to consent to this: he had made his declaration on arriving as an American officer; he had not been authorized by Congress to accept the commission that was offered; and, finally, he felt that it would be dishonorable and disadvantageous, as much as for himself as for America, to switch flags, especially in view of the circumstances. Except for the frigate *Alliance*, all the commodore's squadron belonged to His Most Christian Majesty, and the ambassador of France consequently had the right to dispose of it. The American minister at Paris sent an order to the commodore to deliver all of his prisoners to the ambassador of France, and to obey this instruction the commodore was also forced to deliver to him the *Serapis* and the *Countess of Scarborough* because the other ships could not hold the great number of prisoners.

The commodore continued, therefore, to display the American flag on board the *Alliance*, and as soon as the wind permitted, the vice admiral, after having already made the commodore's sojourn in the Texel as disagreeable as he could, compelled him to set sail in this frigate. The commodore had the good fortune to escape the greediness of the enemy, and the English were so enraged because of that, and also because the States General had granted an escort for the fleet that carried the naval stores from Texel to Brest, that they declared war against the United Provinces a short time later. They listed the stay and conduct of the commodore in the Texel as the first article of their declaration.

These facts were well known by the public throughout Europe; and my motive for giving this testimony to America on behalf of the commodore proceeds from the desire to do justice to his zeal and good conduct, for the honor and interest of the United States in affairs which have come immediately under my own cognizance.

At The Hague, March 10, 1784

(Signed)   E. J. Van Berckel

I, the undersigned, not only certify the exact truth of all before this but, having been officially present on the American squadron in the roads of the Texel for nearly three months, I testify with pleasure.

At The Hague, March 11, 1784

Signed, C. W. F. Dumas, agent of the United States of America

[Translation]

———◆◆◆———

Copy of the letter from the United States of America to His Most Christian Majesty

Great and beloved Friend,

We the United States of America in Congress assembled, in consideration of the distinguished Marks of approbation with which your Majesty has been pleased to honor the Chevalier Paul-Jones as well as from a sense of his Merit, have *unanimously* directed a Medal of Gold to be struck and presented to him, in Commemoration of his Valor and brillant services, while Commanding a Squadron of French and American Ships, under our Flag and Commission off the Coast of Great Britain in the late War.

As it is his earnest Desire to acquire greater Knowledge in his Profession we cannot forbear requesting the Favor of your Majesty to permit him to embark with your Fleets of Evolution, where only it will probably be in his Power to acquire that Degree of Knowledge which may hereafter render him more extensively useful.

Permit us to repeat to your Majesty our sincere assurances, that the various & important Benefits for which we are indebted to your Friendship, will never cease to interest us in whatever may concern the Happiness of your Majesty, your Family and People.

We pray God to keep you, our great & beloved Friend, under his holy Protection.

Done at the City of New-York the Sixteenth Day of October, in the year of our Lord one thousand seven hundred and eighty-seven and of our Sovereignty and Independence the twelfth.

(Signed) ⎰Arthur St. Clair, President
          ⎱John Jay, Secretary for foreign affairs

BIOGRAPHICAL GLOSSARY

ALEXANDER, WILLIAM, JR. (1729–1819): Scottish trader who came to France in 1776; kinsman of Benjamin Franklin and his neighbor in France; secret agent, 1777–78, for Sir William Pulteney, who tried to bring peace through personal negotiations with Franklin; became a merchant in Richmond, Va.

BEAUVAU, CHARLES JUSTE, MARÉCHAL DE (1720–1793): born at Lunéville; captain of the French king's guards, 1756; governor of Provence, 1782.

BERKEL, ENGELBERT F. VAN (1726–1796): grand pensionary of Amsterdam and younger brother of Pieter (first minister from the Netherlands to the United States).

BURBANK, JOHN: master at arms on the *Bonhomme Richard* whose battle assignment was to guard the British prisoners below decks; the logbook of the *Serapis* for September 26, 1779, states that after the battle "that Master at Arms was put in Irons for letting the Prisoners loose on the Night of the Engagement."

BURDON, GEORGE: superannuated British naval officer serving on coastal patrol; not to be confused with Lt. George Burdon, who commanded HMS *West Florida* in Lake Pontchartrain in 1778 and the sloop *Fortune* in 1781.

BYRON, JOHN (1723–1786): vice admiral, British navy; reinforced Lord Howe off North America in 1778–79.

CALONNE, CHARLES ALEXANDRE DE (1734–1802): minister of finance in France, 1783–87.

CAPELLEN TOT DEN POL, JOAN DERK, BARON VAN DER (1741–1784): of Zevolle; member of the House of Nobles of the province of Overÿssel; philosophical leader of the patriot party in the United Provinces; friend of the American Revolution and an unofficial advisor to John Adams when he was minister to the United Provinces.

CARLETON, GUY (1724–1808): 1st lord Dorchester; British general; governor of Quebec, 1775–78 and 1786–96; commander in chief of the British forces in America, 1782–83; he and his main army were stationed at New York.

CASTRIES, CHARLES EUGÈNE GABRIEL DE LA CROIX, MARQUIS DE (1727–1801): appointed minister of marine, 1780; maréchal de France, 1783.

CHAUMONT, JACQUES DONATIEN LE RAY DE (1725–1803): French merchant and shipowner; successively served as a member of the French king's Privy Council, as the king's commissioner for unofficial aid to America, as speculator in contracts for military supplies and the outfitting of American naval vessels, and as paymaster of Jones' squadron.

CLYMER, GEORGE (1739–1813): Philadelphia merchant; member of the Continental Congress, 1776–77 and 1780–82.

CORNWALLIS, CHARLES (1738–1805): 2d earl and 1st marquis Cornwallis; British army general in America, 1776–81; surrendered British southern army at Yorktown, October 19, 1781; later famous as governor-general of India.

COTTINEAU DE KERLOGUEN, DENIS NICOLAS (d. 1808): French naval officer, commanded *la Pallas*; Philadelphia resident after the war.

CULLAM, DAVID (d. 1785?): Portsmouth, N.H., seaman; master on board the *Ranger* and a leader of an attempted mutiny; settled in Portsmouth after the war.

DAER, LORD; see Hamilton, Basil William

DALE, RICHARD (1756–1826): Virginia merchant mariner; lieutenant, Virginia state navy, 1776; midshipman on the frigate *Lexington* and prisoner in Mill Prison, England, 1777–79; 1st lieutenant on the *Bonhomme Richard*, the *Alliance*, 1779–80, and the *Trumbull*, 1781; after a stint on privateers, he returned to the merchant marine.

DEANE, SILAS (1737–1789): Connecticut lawyer-merchant; member of the Continental Congress, 1774–76, and its agent and commissioner in France, 1776–78.

DORSET, LORD; see Sackville, John Frederick

DUMAS, CHARLES GUILLAUME FRÉDÉRIC (1721–1796): born in Germany of French parents, lived in Switzerland but moved to The Hague in 1756 where he wrote for his livelihood; secret agent for America after 1775, advisor and secretary to John Adams at The Hague and American agent at The Hague until 1793.

DUNMORE, LORD; see Murray, John

FRANKLIN, BENJAMIN (1706–1790): native of Massachusetts; scientist, printer, propagandist, and diplomat; American commissioner to France, 1776–85.

FREEMAN, DAVID: probably a former Irish indentured servant and blacksmith from Worcester and Leominster, Mass.; signed on the *Ranger* at Portsmouth, N.H.

GARDNER, HENRY: native of Scotland; acting gunner on the *Bonhomme Richard*. John Connor is also listed on the roster (July 26, 1779) as gunner on the *Bonhomme Richard*, but Gardner is usually credited with giving alarm. Gardner was wounded when Jones hit his head with a pistol butt for calling for quarter.

GARNIER, CHARLES JEAN (1738–1783): French foreign service agent and secretary to the French ambassador in England at the outset of the American Revolution; regarded as an expert on British affairs; considered as a possible successor to Conrad Alexandre Gérard as minister to America, 1779.

GATES, HORATIO (1728–1806): former British army officer, settled in Virginia in 1772; American brigadier general and adjutant general, 1775–76; major general and commander of the Northern Department, 1777–78, the Eastern Department, 1778–79, and the Southern Department, 1780.

GILLON, ALEXANDER (1741–1794): Dutch merchant from Charleston, S.C.; commodore in the South Carolina navy, 1778; South Carolina's agent at Amsterdam to secure a state loan; commanded the *South Carolina* (l'*Indienne*), which took several prizes and participated in the capture of the Bahamas in 1782.

GRAND, FERDINAND: French banker who handled the American accounts in Paris; had a country seat in Passy near Franklin's residence at the Hôtel de Valentinois.

GREENE, NATHANAEL (1742–1786): iron foundry owner from Rhode Island; brigadier general and major general, Continental army; division commander under George Washington, 1775–78, 1780; quartermaster general, 1778–80; commander of the Southern Department, 1780–83.

GUNNISON, JOHN: listed along with Joseph Collison and Jacques Connou as carpenter on the *Bonhomme Richard*.

HALL, ELIJAH: shipbuilder and merchant from Portsmouth, N.H.; 2d lieutenant on the *Ranger*; commanded the *Drake* as a prize ship.

HAMILTON, BASIL WILLIAM, LORD DAER (1763–1794): second son of Dunbar Hamilton, Lord Selkirk; sympathizer with the French Revolution while in Paris, 1789–90.

HAMILTON, DUNBAR (1722–1799): earl of Selkirk; representative peer from Scotland, 1787–99.

HAZARD, JOHN: 1st lieutenant on the *Katy*, 1775; captain of the *Providence*; the first officer cashiered from the Continental navy.

HEWES, JOSEPH (1730–1779): merchant and politician from Edenton, N.C.; member of the Continental Congress, 1774–76, 1779; served on the Marine Committee.

HOOD, SAMUEL (1724–1816): 1st viscount Hood; career officer in the British navy; commissioner of the Portsmouth dockyard, 1778–80; rear admiral, second in command to Rodney, in the West Indies, 1781–82.

HOPKINS, ESEK (1718–1802): native of Rhode Island; commanded a privateer during the French and Indian War; commander in chief of the Continental navy, 1775–77; brother of Stephen (1707–1785), a member of the Marine Committee of the Continental Congress.

HOUSTON, WILLIAM C. (1746–1788): tutor and professor at the College of New Jersey, 1769–83; lawyer in Trenton; member of the Continental Congress, 1779–81 and 1784–85.

HOWE, RICHARD (1726–1799): 4th viscount and first earl Howe; British admiral, commander in chief of British forces in North America, 1776–78.

HUMPHREYS, DAVID (1752–1818): native of Connecticut; aide-de-camp to Israel Putnam and Nathanael Greene, 1778–80, and to George Washington, 1780–83; secretary to the Commission for Negotiating Commercial Treaties with Foreign Powers, 1784–86, in France and England; U.S. agent and minister, 1790–1801, in Africa and Europe.

HUNTINGTON, SAMUEL (1731–1796): lawyer from Norwich, Conn.; member of the Continental Congress, 1776–84, president, 1779–81; governor of Connecticut, 1786–96.

JACKSON, JOHN (d. 1836): English pilot from the Humber; detained by Jones and lost an arm during the battle with the *Serapis*; given about $250 by Jones but never received his pension.

JAY, JOHN (1745–1829): New York lawyer; member of the Continental Congress, 1774–76 and 1778–79, president, 1778–79; minister to Spain, 1779–83; peace commissioner to England, 1782–83; secretary of foreign affairs, 1784–89.

LAFAYETTE, MARIE JOSEPH PAUL YVES ROCH GILBERT DU MOTIER, MARQUIS DE (1757–1834): French nobleman and army officer; commissioned as a major general in the American army at age 19; commanded an American army in the Virginia campaign, 1780–81, that kept pressure on Cornwallis until the main army moved against Yorktown; confidant of Washington.

LA LUZERNE, ANNE CÉSAR, CHEVALIER DE (1714–1791): French ambassador to Bavaria, 1776–79; minister plenipotentiary to the United States, 1779–87.

LA MOTTE-PICQUET DE LA VINOYÈRE; see Piquet De La Motte, Comte Toussaint-Guillaume

LANDAIS, PIERRE (1734–1820): born in St. Malo, France; served in the French navy and on the Bougainville expedition, 1766–69; captain of the frigate Alliance, 1778; suspended from command by Franklin in 1779; resumed his command with the encouragement of Arthur Lee, 1780; his conduct was highly eccentric and after an investigation he was dismissed from the U.S. Navy.

LA TOUCHE-TRÉVILLE, LOUIS RENÉ MAGDELAIN LAVASSOR, VICOMTE DE (1745–1804): French naval captain; commander of l'Hermione; stationed at Boston, 1780.

LA VAUGUYON, PAUL FRANÇOIS DE QUÉLEN DE STUER DE CAUSSADE, DUC DE (1746–1828): French ambassador at The Hague, 1776–83; ambassador to Spain, 1784–89.

LEE, ARTHUR (1740–1792): Virginian and brother of Richard Henry Lee; active in the pamphlet warfare in the 1770's while still living in London; commissioner to France and Spain, 1776–79; member of the Continental Congress, 1781–84.

LEGRAND, FERDINAND; see Grand, Ferdinand

LUNT, CUTTING (1749–1780?): native of Newburyport, Mass.; seaman on the Alfred and the Providence with his cousin Henry Lunt, 1775–76; captured while on a privateer and confined to Mill Prison, England, 1776–79; master and 3d lieutenant on the Bonhomme Richard.

LUNT, HENRY (1753–1805): native of Newburyport, Mass.; served on the Alfred and the Providence and was prisoner in England, 1776–79; 2d lieutenant on the Bonhomme Richard and then on the Alliance.

MACCARTHY, EUGENE ROBERT (1757–1801): native of County Kerry, Ireland; French army cadet, 1772–75; sous-lieutenant, Régiment de Walsh-Serrant, 1776; lieutenant en seconde, 1779; promoted to captain and awarded 400 livres, December 12, 1779, for service with Jones; later served at Tobago and St. Christopher.

MCDOUGALL, ALEXANDER (1732–1786): New York merchant and patriot leader; Continental army brigadier general, 1776, major general, 1777–83; member of the Continental Congress, 1781.

MALESHERBES, CHRÉTIEN GUILLAUME DE LAMOIGNON DE (1721–1794): president of the cours des aides, 1750–55; member of the council of state under Louis XVI, 1775–76 and 1787–88.

MATHEWS, JOHN (1744–1802): South Carolina lawyer, legislator, and judge; member of the Continental Congress, 1778–81.

MAUREPAS, JEAN FRÉDÉRIC PHÉLIPPEAUX, COMTE DE (1701–1781): son of the French secretary of state for the marine and the royal household, a post to which he succeeded in 1715; minister of state under Louis XVI, 1738–49.

MEASE, MATTHEW (d. 1787): perhaps the native of Ireland who emigrated to Pennsylvania and became a Philadelphia shipowner by 1775; served as ship's purser on the Bonhomme Richard and on l'Ariel.

MONTBARREY, ALEXANDRE-MARIE-LÉONOR DE SAINT-MAURICE, PRINCE DE (1732–1796): commander of the king's house guards, Cent-Suisses, 1763; minister of war, 1777–80.

MONTMORRES, HERVEY REDMOND MORRES (1743–1797): viscount, Irish peer.

MORGAN, DANIEL (1736–1802): frontier farmer and land speculator; commanded Virginia Rifle Company at Boston and Quebec, 1775; commanded 11th Virginia Regiment, 1777–79; commanded Light Infantry Brigade, 1780–81, and defeated British at the battle of Cowpens.

MORRIS, ROBERT (1734–1806): English-born Philadelphia merchant; member of the Continental Congress, 1775–78; superintendent of finance, 1781–84.

MORTON, KATHERIN, COUNTESS OF: wife of Sholto Charles, 16th earl of Morton, and sister of Lord Selkirk's wife Helen; daughter of John Hamilton, son of the 6th earl of Haddington.

MOYLAN, JAMES: former Philadelphia merchant and brother of Stephen (a Philadelphia merchant and muster master general, 1775–76, and quartermaster general, 1776, of the Continental Army); merchant and U.S. commercial agent at Lorient; partner of M. Gourlade at Morlaix; procured the Bonhomme Richard for Jones.

113

MURRAY, JOHN (1732–1809): 4th earl of Dunmore; royal governor of New York, 1770–71, and Virginia, 1771–75.

NASSAU-SIEGEN, CHARLES-HENRI-NICOLAS-OTHON, PRINCE DE (1745–1809): relative of the prince of Orange; international adventurer; squadron commander in the Russian navy, 1788; commanded the Baltic flotilla of the Russian navy after forcing Jones out of that country.

NESBITT, JONATHAN: merchant-banker at Lorient; brother of John M. Nesbitt, Philadelphia merchant and revolutionary leader.

O'KELLY, JAMES GERARD: sublieutenant in the Régiment de Walsh-Serrant; killed in action during the battle between the Bonhomme Richard and HMS Serapis.

ORVILLIERS, LOUIS GUILLOUET, COMTE D' (1708–1792): French admiral; commanded fleet at Brest and led the combined French-Spanish fleet that assembled in 1779 to attack Plymouth, England, but failed to complete its mission.

OSGOOD, SAMUEL (1748–1813): merchant from Massachusetts; member of the Continental Congress, 1781–84; commissioner of the U.S. Treasury, 1785–89; U.S. Postmaster, 1789–91.

PARKER, PETER (1721–1811): commanded small English squadron going to America in October 1775; defeated at Charleston, June 1776; participated in British victories in New York, Rhode Island, and the West Indies.

PEARSON, RICHARD (1731–1806): native of Westmoreland, England; served in the British navy, 1745–50, 1755–90, and commanded a ship from 1770; commanded the Serapis from March 1778; commanded the Arethusa off North America, 1781–82.

PIERCY, THOMAS (d. 1783): appointed lieutenant in the royal navy in 1757, promoted to commander in 1778 and to captain in 1780.

PIGOT, HUGH (1721?–1792): veteran English naval officer; commander of the West Indies fleet, 1782–83.

PINDAR, JOHN: New York loyalist; former pilot for the British navy at Sandy Hook; captain of the British privateer Triumph of 20 guns (the former Massachusetts privateer Tracy).

PIQUET DE LA MOTTE, COMTE TOUSSAINT-GUILLAUME (1720–1791); commanded small escort squadron on convoy duty off the French coast, 1778; captured Admiral Rodney's treasure convoy from St. Eustatius, 1781.

RAYNAL, GUILLAUME THOMAS FRANÇOIS (1713–1796): French philosopher and writer known as Abbé Raynal; author of Histoire philosophique et politique des établissemens et du commerce des Européens dans les deux Indes (1770).

RICOT, PHILIPPE NICOLAS: French naval lieutenant and U.S. Navy captain; commanded la Vengeance of 12 guns.

RIEMERSMA, NICOLAAS: Dutch naval captain ordinaris; acting naval commander in the Texel when Jones arrived; later commanded the squadron that brought Pieter van Berckel, first Dutch minister to America, to Boston.

ROCHAMBEAU, JEAN BAPTISTE DONATIEN DE VIMEUR, COMTE DE (1725–1807): native of Vendôme; served in the French army from 1743; commanded the French expeditionary army in America, 1780–83; maréchal de France and army commander in Europe.

RODNEY, GEORGE BRYDGES (1719–1792): 1st baron Rodney; British admiral; served in the English navy from 1732; commander in chief of the Leeward Islands station, 1779–82; defeated the Spanish at Cape St. Vincent, 1780, and the French in the battle off Saints Passage, 1782.

SACKVILLE, JOHN FREDERICK (1745–1799): 3d duke of Dorset; captain of the yeoman of the guard, 1782–83; ambassador-extraordinary and plenipotentiary to France, 1783–89; lord lieutenant of Kent, 1769–97.

SAINT-SIMON, CLAUDE-ANNE, MARQUIS DE (1740–1819): French army officer after 1758; commanded the regiments of Poitiers, 1771–75, and of Touraine, 1775–79; commanded Spanish force of 2,000 men in America, 1780–83; governor of St.Jean-Pied-de-Port; Spanish general after the French Revolution.

SALTONSTALL, DUDLEY (1738–1796): Connecticut native and brother-in-law of Silas Deane; commanded the Alfred, 1775, the frigate Trumbull, 1777–78, the frigate Warren, 1778–79, the naval forces in the Penobscot expedition, 1779, and the privateer Minerva, 1781; dismissed from the U.S. Navy in 1779 after the American defeat at Penobscot Bay.

SARTINE, ANTOINE-RAYMOND-JEAN-GUALBERT-GABRIEL DE (1729–1801): French minister of the marine, 1774–80.

SÉGUR, PHILIPPE HENRI, MARQUIS DE (1724–1801): maréchal de camp and lieutenant general in the French army; minister of war, 1780–87.

SELKIRK, EARL OF; see Hamilton, Dunbar

SELKIRK, LADY HELEN: daughter of John Hamilton (second son of the 6th earl of Haddington), wife of Dunbar Hamilton, and sister of Katherine, countess of Morton.

SERRANT, JOSEPH PHILIPPE WALSH, COMTE DE (1744–1817): born at Cadix; proprietary colonel of the former Régiment de Roscommon, one of five Irish regiments, in 1770; maréchal de camp, 1784.

SHARPE, WILLIAM (1742–1818): North Carolina lawyer, member of the Continental Congress, 1779–81.

SIMPSON, THOMAS: native of Portsmouth, N.H., and brother-in-law of John Langdon; merchant mariner; commanded the privateer *Alexander* and the *Ranger*, from 1778 until captured off Charleston, 1780.

STACK, EDWARD (1756–1833): native of County Kerry, Ireland; French Army cadet, 1770; sous-lieutenant, 1772; went with Lafayette to America as lieutenant, 1777; 1st lieutenant, 1779; commissioned captain and awarded 400 livres for service with Jones, December 12, 1779.

SULLIVAN, JOHN (1740–1795): New Hampshire lawyer; Continental army brigadier general, 1775, major general, 1776–79; member of the Continental Congress, 1774–75 and 1780–81; president of New Hampshire, 1786–90.

THÉVENARD, ANTOINE-JEAN-MARIE, COMTE (1733–1815): French vice admiral; succeeded M. de Grandville as captain of the port of Lorient.

THIERRY DE LA PRÉVALAYE, PIERRE DEMAS, MARQUIS (1745–1816): artillery officer; served on *la Nymphe* and *l'Actif*, 1778, *l'Orient* and *la Ville de Paris*, 1779–80, *le Saint Esprit* and *la Bretagne*, 1780–81, and *l'Astrée*, 1783.

THOMSON, CHARLES (1729–1824): Philadelphia merchant and patriot leader; secretary of the Continental Congress, 1774–89.

VARNUM, JAMES M. (1748–1789): Rhode Island lawyer; member of the Continental Congress, 1780–82 and 1786–87; U.S. judge for the Northwest Territory, 1787–89.

VAUDREUIL, LOUIS PHILIPPE RIGAUD, MARQUIS DE (1723–1802): French naval officer from 1741; commanded squadron at St. Louis, Senegal, 1779; commanded 15-vessel squadron in the West Indies expedition, 1782–83.

VERGENNES, CHARLES GRAVIER, COMTE DE (1717–1787): native of Dijon, France; French ambassador at Treves, Constantinople, and Stockholm; foreign minister of France under Louis XVI.

VIOMÉNIL, JOSEPH HYACINTHE DU HOUX (1734–1827): French army officer; became maréchal de camp in 1780; served under Rochambeau and in the American theater to 1783.

WALLINGFORD, SAMUEL (1755–1778): lieutenant, U.S. Marine Corps; killed on board the *Ranger* in the battle with the *Drake*.

WASHINGTON, GEORGE (1732–1799): Virginia planter; member of the Continental Congress, 1774–75; commander in chief of the American army, 1775–83; U.S. President, 1789–97.

WAYNE, ANTHONY (1745–1796): tanner in Pennsylvania; brigadier general and commander of the Pennsylvania Line, 1777–83; commander of the Light Infantry Brigade, 1779; commanded an American army in Ohio, 1792–96.

WILLIAMSON, HUGH (1735–1819): doctor in Philadelphia to 1773; merchant in North Carolina after 1776; surgeon general of North Carolina troops, 1779–82; member of the Continental Congress, 1782–85 and 1788; U.S. Congress, 1789–93.

YORKE, JOSEPH (1724–1792): Baron Dover, son of the earl of Hardwicke; British minister at The Hague, 1751–60; ambassador, 1761–80.

ADVISORY COMMITTEE

Library of Congress American Revolution Bicentennial Program

John R. Alden
James B. Duke Professor of History Emeritus, Duke University

Julian P. Boyd
Editor of The Papers of Thomas Jefferson, *Princeton University*

Lyman H. Butterfield
Editor in Chief Emeritus of The Adams Papers, *Massachusetts Historical Society*

Jack P. Greene
Andrew W. Mellon Professor in the Humanities, The Johns Hopkins University

Merrill Jensen
Editor of The Documentary History of the Ratification of the Constitution

Cecelia M. Kenyon
Charles N. Clark Professor of Government, Smith College

Aubrey C. Land
University Research Professor, University of Georgia

Edmund S. Morgan
Sterling Professor of History, Yale University

Richard B. Morris
Gouverneur Morris Professor of History Emeritus, Columbia University

George C. Rogers, Jr.
Yates Snowden Professor of American History, University of South Carolina

Note: When the project to translate this memoir was initiated, Whitfield J. Bell, Jr., Librarian of the American Philosophical Society, and Adrienne Koch, Professor of American Intellectual History at the University of Maryland, were members of the advisory committee. Professor Koch died in 1971 and Mr. Bell resigned in 1973.

116

☆ U.S. GOVERNMENT PRINTING OFFICE : 1979 O—252-414

emparé de tout l'argent qui étoit provenu de la vente de mes prises marchandes; et après avoir écrit des volumes de lettres pour réclamer l'argent des prises et de la solde, ne pouvant obtenir satisfaction ni pour les officiers, ni pour les .... me rendis à la Cour pour y demander justice.

Le Docteur Franklin m'accompagna à Versailles, et le Ministre de la Marine, sur notre demande, donna des ordres pour la vente des prises. Quoiqu'il fut évident que j'avois souffert par les fatigues peu communes que j'avois éprouvées, n'ayant pas dormi trois heures dans 24 durant toute la Campagne depuis Lorient jusqu'au Texel; le Ministre cependant me reçus avec beaucoup de froid, et il ne me demanda pas même si je ne ressentois des mauvais effets des blessures que j'avois reçues.

En conséquence je ne demandai pas au Ministre de me présenter au Roi; mais j'allai avec le Docteur Franklin au lever de Sa Majesté, et le lendemain M. le Prince de Beauveau Capitaine des Gardes me fit l'honneur de me présenter plus particulièrement à Sa Majesté.